FROM
BONDAGE
TO
FREEDOM

FROM
BONDAGE
TO
FREEDOM

*A Survey of Jewish History
from the Babylonian Captivity
to the Coming of the Messiah*

DANIEL FUCHS
HAROLD A. SEVENER

FROM BONDAGE TO FREEDOM
© 1995 by Chosen People Ministries Inc.

Unless otherwise noted,
Scripture quotations in this book are taken from the
HOLY BIBLE: NEW INTERNATIONAL VERSION ®. NIV ®.
Copyright © 1973, 1978, 1984 by International Bible Society.
Used by permission of Zondervan Publishing House.
The "NIV" and "New International Version" trademarks
are registered in the United States Patent and Trademark Office
by International Bible Society.

Verses marked (KJV) are taken from the King James version.

Quotations from THE LIFE OF GREECE by Will Durant
are reprinted with the permission of Simon & Schuster.
Copyright © 1939 by Will Durant.
Copyright renewed 1967 by Will Durant.

Quotations from JEWS, GOD AND HISTORY,
REVISED AND UPDATED EDITION by Max I. Dimont
are used by permission of Dutton Signet,
a division of Penguin Books USA Inc.
Copyright © 1962, renewed 1990 by Max I. Dimont.
Copyright © 1994 by Ethel Dimont.

Library of Congress Cataloging-in-Publication Data

Fuchs, Daniel, 1911-
From bondage to freedom: a survey of Jewish history from the
Babylonian Captivity to the coming of the Messiah /
Daniel Fuchs, Harold A. Sevener.
Includes bibliographical references.
ISBN 0-87213-199-8 (pbk.)
1. Jews—History—586 B.C.–70 A.D. 2. Judaism—History—Post-exilic
period, 586 B.C.–210 A.D.
I. Sevener, Harold A. II. Title.
DS121.65.F83 1995
909'.04924—dc20   95-45158

Printed in the United States of America
10 9 8 7 6 5 4 3 2 1

Contents

Foreword

F rom *Bondage to Freedom* was originally titled "From the Exile to the Christ" and appeared in serial form in *The Chosen People* magazine, a monthly publication of Chosen People Ministries Inc.

The series was begun by the late Dr. Daniel Fuchs, then chairman of the Board of Directors of Chosen People Ministries Inc., in response to a number of requests for concise information and historical detail concerning the intertestamental period: the so-called four hundred silent years. It was Dr. Fuchs's desire to see this series in book form so that the information would be readily available to Christians and those interested in the history of the Jewish people.

However, Dr. Fuchs was called home to be with the Lord before he was able to finish the series. His wife Muriel and the Board of Directors of Chosen People Ministries Inc. then asked me to finish his excellent study and edit the entire manuscript.

From Bondage to Freedom is the product of that labor. The book is lovingly dedicated to the memory of Dr. Daniel Fuchs, whose desire was that his readers would gain further knowledge of the world into which our Messiah was born and a greater understanding of the Jewish people.

Harold A. Sevener
President Emeritus
Chosen People Ministries Inc.
Charlotte, North Carolina

Introduction

I n our Bibles there is a blank page between the Old
Testament and the New Testament. The casual reader
quickly turns this blank page and does not realize
that it represents four hundred years of history. This
period of time is equal to all of the years between the
discovery of America in 1492 and the beginning of the
twentieth century.

Because of the fact that during the intertestamental
period no prophet arose and no inspired historian added
to the Scriptures, many students call these years the "four
silent centuries." This terminology is unfortunate. God
was not silent *about* them. Their history is prophesied
minutely in the prophecy of Daniel. Much of the story is
also foretold in Isaiah and Jeremiah. God was also not
silent *during* these years. In remarkable ways He not only
preserved His people, but also prepared the world for
the coming of the promised Messiah.

One cannot fully understand the relationship of the
Old Testament and the New Testament without learning
about the history of the intervening years. The era was
one of substantial change. The Old Testament closes with
the Jews ruled by Persia; the New Testament opens with
the Jews governed by Rome. In the Old Testament we
read that the Jewish people frequently became idolaters;
in the New Testament we read of Pharisees, Sadducees,
and Zealots, but not idolaters. Synagogues are hardly
mentioned in the Old Testament, but they are mentioned
frequently in the New Testament. The Old Testament was
written mostly in Hebrew; the New Testament was written

in Greek. These facts are not trivial; they indicate that during the "silent" era God was moving forward in accomplishing His purpose to fulfill His promise to Abraham.

The scope of our study is *from the exile to the Messiah.* These words are taken from Matthew 1:17: "There were fourteen generations in all from Abraham to David, fourteen from David to the exile to Babylon, and fourteen *from the exile to the Christ* [Messiah]" (italics added). The three periods are not just subdivisions; they are an outline of Jewish history:

A. From Abraham to David:
   The Era of Promise
B. From David to the Exile to Babylon:
   The Era of Failure
C. From the Exile to the Christ:
   The Era of Preparation for the Messiah

This study deals with history. There will be dates mentioned (not too many), people named, and wars described. But it is not our purpose to write an almanac. Our purpose is to give an account of the acts of God as He demonstrated His power in the control of history.

It has been the purpose of God to offer salvation to all men everywhere. Man failed, but God still pursued His purpose. He finally chose a single family to whom He entrusted His promises, in order that eventually the whole world would have the opportunity to receive His grace. This family grew into the nation of Israel. They were called by God for His purpose, and apart from His purpose there is no understanding of their history.

The modern philosopher of history simply cannot understand their persistence as a people. Arnold Toynbee, who wrote the imposing twelve-volume *A Study of History,* realized that the Jews did not fit into his theories, so he ignored the Jewish people. He thought their nation should have disappeared soon after they went into exile. But they did not die, and the reason is that the God of Abraham, Isaac, and Jacob still lives and He promised to

Abraham that "all peoples on earth will be blessed through you" (Genesis 12:3).

In preparation for this study you may want to read the books of 1 Kings and 2 Kings at *one sitting*. The history recorded in these books covers what Matthew called "from David to the exile to Babylon" and what we named "the era of failure."

These books were written sometime during that exile. According to Jewish tradition, they were written by Jeremiah. We cannot be certain about his authorship, but there is internal evidence that he could have written at least part of them.

The author of 1 and 2 Kings was not merely writing a history. He had an important message. The message is clear. William Sanford LaSor said it is to show that Israel

> ...the total nation—as the people of Yahweh [Jehovah[1]] is expected to keep the law of Yahweh, particularly the purity of worship of Yahweh, and that there is blessing in so doing, and punishment for failure to keep His law.
>
> Since the king stands in the place of the nation, the author has chosen to proclaim his message principally by telling the story of the kings. It is noteworthy that each king's reign is judged not on political grounds but on religious grounds alone: he "did what was evil in the sight of Yahweh," or "he did what was right in the eyes of Yahweh." Perhaps the most striking example of this is Omri of Israel, by political measure one of the greatest kings of Israel, who is dismissed with eight verses and summarized in the statement, "Omri did what was evil in the sight of Yahweh, and did more evil than all who were before him."[2]

The story of Israel's decline "from David to the exile" began early in this period. It was not long before King Solomon, who had been "greater in riches and wisdom than all the other kings of the earth" (1 Kings 10:23), was led astray by his seven hundred wives and three hundred concubines. "He followed Ashtoreth the goddess of the Sidonians, and Molech the detestable god of the Ammonites. So Solomon did evil in the eyes of the Lord" (11:5-6).

God had given the Abrahamic covenant so that in Abraham's seed "all peoples on the earth will be blessed" and now the seed of Abraham and David introduced the gods of the nations into his own home! The idolatry of Solomon's household became the scourge of Israel and Judah. Solomon never denied that Jehovah was God. He tacitly acknowledged that Jehovah was the God of the Hebrews, but he also gave the gods of the Moabites, Ammonites, Edomites, Sidonites, and Hittites validity. In effect he baptized their paganism and "the Lord became angry with Solomon" (1 Kings 11:9). Solomon's son Rehoboam did not listen to what his father *said;* he copied his *acts* and the eventual result was the exile.

The downward trend was temporarily stopped during the reign of Josiah, who ruled in Judah more than three centuries after Solomon. Under Josiah's leadership the temple was repaired in 621 B.C. During the repairs his workmen discovered a scroll of "the Book of the Law" (2 Kings 22:8), evidently Deuteronomy, which had been stored in the temple and forgotten. After the scroll was read to Josiah, he called together all the elders of Jerusalem and solemnly pledged to obey God's covenant.

King Josiah inaugurated a reform. The reformation began in Jerusalem and spread throughout Judah. All of the idols and artifacts connected with Assyrian worship were destroyed and the observance of Passover was renewed. It is important to understand that this reformation was carried out in obedience to the written Word of God. However, the reformation did not last long. Before the end of the century the nation once more apostatized into the idolatry that eventually led to the exile.

There was another highly significant movement during "the era of failure." In the last half of the eighth century B.C. the *writing* prophets began to play a leading part in Israel's history. Foremost among them was Isaiah.

He was a statesman-prophet who ministered to a number of Judah's kings. At times he persuaded the kings to obey God, but the general trend was downward. King Ahaz rejected Isaiah's advice and entered into an alliance with Assyria. The Assyrians, as a result, oppressed Israel for more than a century.

During the declining years of Judah, the prophet Jeremiah warned the people of imminent judgment for their sins. He foretold the captivity, but also prophesied the restoration. He reminded them of God's faithfulness to the covenant and foretold the new covenant, which would last forever through the Messiah. But in spite of all of God's graciousness, sin resulted in national decay and finally the people were led into captivity.

During the reign of Jehoiakim, Nebuchadnezzar invaded the land of the Jews and carried many of them to Babylon. Among the captives was Daniel. Seven years later, in 598 B.C., ten thousand more of the people were forcibly removed by Nebuchadnezzar. Among these were King Jehoiakim and the prophet Ezekiel.

In 586 B.C. when Zedekiah spurned the advice of Jeremiah, Nebuchadnezzar took Jerusalem, destroyed the temple, carried the upper classes to Babylon, and left only the poorer of the people to till the land. It was a terrible day. The city where Solomon reigned in all his glory was leveled to the ground and while the Babylonians ravaged the city, the Edomites reviled the descendants of Jacob. An anonymous psalmist wrote:

> Remember, O Lord, what the Edomites did
>   on the day Jerusalem fell.
> "Tear it down," they cried,
>   "tear it down to its foundations!"
> O Daughter of Babylon, doomed to destruction,
>   happy is he who repays you
>   for what you have done to us—
> he who seizes your infants
>   and dashes them against the rocks.
>   (Psalm 137:7-9)

It looked as if Jewish history had ended. But God had promised Abraham, "All peoples on earth will be blessed through you." At ease in Zion, Israel kept God's promises for themselves; but exiled to Babylon and from there dispersed to the uttermost parts of the earth, the Jewish people changed. They learned to abhor idolatry and bless their pagan neighbors.

It was during the intertestamental period that God used the dispersed Jewish nation as His witnesses. They translated the Hebrew Scriptures into Greek so that all nations could know Him. It was God's missionary program to all nations, "to the Jew first and also to the Gentile" (Romans 2:10, KJV).

When Nebuchadnezzar attacked Jerusalem, he "removed all the treasures from the temple of the Lord and from the royal palace, and took away all the gold articles that Solomon king of Israel had made for the temple of the Lord" (2 Kings 24:13). Nebuchadnezzar took these treasures to Babylon. But the Jewish nation, by God's grace, had a greater treasure: the written Word of God.

It was the custom for victorious ancient nations to systematically scatter the people of the countries they conquered by enforced emigration. This ruse kept the people from uniting in a common rebellion. For example 136 years before the Babylonian captivity, the Assyrian kings had taken the ten tribes of Israel far to the north and northeast. Thus most historians call them the lost tribes. They were lost both physically and spiritually, but the Old and New Testaments clearly teach that they were not lost to God's plans and purposes.

Assyria was in turn conquered by Babylon under Nebuchadnezzar, who adopted the same tactics. In three separate movements from 605–586 B.C. he systematically destroyed the cities of Judah, deported most of the Jewish people, and scattered them in colonies along the Tigris and Euphrates rivers of Babylon.

It was a sad time for the Jews. To many it seemed as if the God of Abraham, Isaac, and Jacob were impotent against the gods of Assyria and Babylon. The mental and spiritual state of the captives was deplorable. Their deportation and the destruction of the temple seemed to be proof that Jehovah was but one of the many gods worshiped in Babylon.

We will never understand the later history of the Jewish people until we visualize the depravity of the Babylonian system. Will Durant, in his monumental work *The Story of Civilization*, described one aspect of the Babylonian society:

> Ishtar [Astarte to the Greeks, Ashtoreth to the Jews] interests us not only as an analogue of the Egyptian Isis and prototype of the Grecian Aphrodite and the Roman Venus, but as the formal beneficiary of one of the strangest of Babylonian customs.
>
> She was Demeter as well as Aphrodite—no mere goddess of physical beauty and love, but the gracious divinity of bounteous motherhood, the secret inspiration of the growing soil, and the creative principle everywhere.
>
> It is impossible to find much harmony, from a modern point of view, in the attributes and functions of Ishtar: she was the goddess of war as well as of love, of prostitutes as well as of mothers; she called herself "a compassionate courtesan"; she was represented sometimes as a bearded bisexual deity, sometimes as a nude female offering her breasts to suck; and though her worshipers repeatedly addressed her as "The Virgin," "The Holy Virgin," and "The Virgin Mother," this merely meant that her amours were free from all taint of wedlock. Gilgamesh rejected her advances on the ground that she could not be trusted; had she not once loved, seduced, and then slain, a lion?
>
> It is clear that we must put our own moral code to one side if we are to understand her. Note with what fervor the Babylonians could lift up to her throne litanies of laudation only less splendid than

those which a tender piety once raised to the Mother
of God:

> I beseech thee, Lady of Ladies,
> Goddess of Goddesses, Ishtar, Queen
> of all cities, leaders of all men.
> Thou art the light of the world,
> thou art the light of heaven.[3]

So much for Ishtar! One historian cited an official cen-
sus of the gods and goddesses worshiped in the ninth
century B.C. The count was sixty-five thousand! Most of
the gods, it was said, lived in temples and made noctur-
nal visits to pious women and helped increase Babylon's
population. There is a famous paragraph in the writings
of Herodotus that begins, "Every native woman is obliged,
once in her life, to sit in the temple of Venus, and have
intercourse with some stranger."[4]

In ancient days defeated peoples and civilizations were
exiled to extinction. They exchanged their defeated gods
for the "superior" gods of their conquerors. This was the
beginning of assimilation. The defeated wanted only to
survive; it didn't matter much to them whether they sur-
vived as Canaanites, Hittites, or Phoenicians. They were
willing to lose their religion or national identity; they
only wanted to live. This is evidently what had happened
to the ten northern tribes of Israel.

Why didn't it happen to Judah? The philosophers of
history have no answers. Arnold Toynbee was so frus-
trated by the persistence of the Jewish people that he
called them a "fossil" nation! It is fascinating to observe
that one of the exiles, Ezekiel, used a similar figure of
speech:

> Then he said to me: "Son of man, these bones
> are the whole house of Israel. They say, 'Our bones
> are dried up and our hope is gone; we are cut off.'
> Therefore prophesy and say to them: 'This is what
> the Sovereign Lord says: O my people, I am going

to open your graves and bring you up from them; I will bring you back to the land of Israel. Then you, my people, will know that I am the Lord, when I open your graves and bring you up from them. I will put my Spirit in you and you will live, and I will settle you in your own land. Then you will know that I the Lord have spoken, and I have done it, declares the Lord'" (Ezekiel 37:11-14).

Why did the Jews persevere in a situation where mightier nations perished? Because fourteen centuries before the exile the Lord had said to Abraham:

Leave your country, your people and your father's household and go to the land I will show you. I will make you into a great nation and I will bless you; I will make your name great, and you will be a blessing. I will bless those who bless you, and whoever curses you I will curse; and all peoples on earth will be blessed through you (Genesis 12:1-3).

It has always been God's will that all men everywhere honor, love, worship, and obey Him. God's purpose in calling Abraham was that all peoples on earth would be blessed through him. When the Jews were exiled to Babylon, their worldwide dispersion and God's missionary program began.

While they occupied their own land, the Jews frequently sinned and lapsed into idolatry, and God sent them one prophet after another. "But they did not listen or pay attention; instead, they followed the stubborn inclinations of their evil hearts. They went backward and not forward" (Jeremiah 7:24). And God punished them.

Arriving in Babylon, the Jews saw idolatry at its worst. Many abandoned their faith in Jehovah and lusted after the goddesses of Babylon. But not all! "By the rivers of Babylon we sat and wept when we remembered Zion" (Psalm 137:1). This remnant remembered the warnings of God's prophets and realized that the exile was God's punishment for the idolatry of the Jewish people. The penitent remnant was transformed; God put iron into their spines. From that time on, although there may have been individual momentary failures, never again did the Jewish nation lapse into idolatry.

When Jews in the twentieth century see Christendom genuflect to what they call an idol, they are reminded of the abomination of Babylonian mysteries. We must show them that this is not Biblical Christianity!

But he who sees the Babylonian exile merely as punishment misses one of the greatest truths of history. Even in the midst of their suffering, God still loved the Jews and remembered His covenant with Abraham. In Babylon and throughout the Babylonian world, wherever they were, the Jews blessed their pagan neighbors. The Jews did not worship idols; they worshiped Jehovah. They honored their fathers and mothers; they also honored and loved their wives and families. They met together on the sabbath and studied the Law and the Prophets. Wherever there was a Jewish community, there was an island of praise to Jehovah in the midst of a sea of immorality. In their adversity, God proved His faithfulness to His Word.

As we study this story of God's faithfulness, we will learn how God dispersed His people throughout the world to areas that became Persia, Greece, Egypt, Syria, and Rome. We will learn how they formed colonies in Rome, Corinth, Galatia, Ephesus, Philippi, Colossae, Thessalonica, and other areas, so that all people everywhere were blessed through them.

We will also see that if the Jews had not been dispersed throughout all nations, the book of Acts and the letters to the Romans, Corinthians, Galatians, Ephesians, Philippians, Colossians, and Thessalonians would never have been written. We will see history's greatest example of how "the Lord disciplines those he loves, and he punishes everyone he accepts as a son" (Hebrews 12:6). Above all we will see that the kings of mighty nations do not control history—the King of kings does!

1

The Prophetic Scriptures and the Exile

O ne of the reasons modern philosophers consider Israel a fossil of history is their a priori tenet that there is no such thing as prophecy. On the other hand, the perseverance of the Jewish people during and after the exile is one of the marvelous proofs of the inspiration of the Scriptures. It vindicates prophecy.

A prophet was a man who spoke for God. Prediction of future events was not the only part of his mission. He spoke for God to Israel about the past, present, and future.

> And we have the word of the prophets made more certain, and you will do well to pay attention to it, as to a light shining in a dark place, until the day dawns and the morning star rises in your hearts. Above all, you must understand that no prophecy of Scripture came about by the prophet's own interpretation. For prophecy never had its origin in the will of man, but *men spoke from God* as they were carried along by the Holy Spirit (2 Peter 1:19-21, italics added).

ISAIAH

We are so accustomed to studying the sublime Messianic prophecies of Isaiah that we often neglect the fact that Isaiah was the first prophet to foretell the exile to Babylon. On two occasions when Judah was threatened by calamity, Isaiah gave wise counsel and foretold the exile: he first prophesied by inference to Ahaz and later gave a plain warning to Hezekiah.

The history of Isaiah's dealings with Ahaz is found in Isaiah 7:1–12:6. This section of the book of Isaiah has been called the "Book of Immanuel." The reader should carefully study this section. Although it is a difficult passage, some facts are clear.

When Ahaz, king of Judah, persisted in making a desperate alliance with Assyria against Syria and Israel, Isaiah vigorously tried to dissuade Ahaz from making the disastrous treaty. The real issue was the choice between faith in God's promise and faith in a human alliance. Ahaz refused to listen to Isaiah and decided to trust Assyria! As a result, because Ahaz rejected God, God rejected Ahaz.

Isaiah then prophesied that a perfect King, Immanuel, would arise "from the stump of Jesse" (Isaiah 11:1). Isaiah was prophesying concerning a historical situation. He was foretelling the coming of the Messiah from David's line. The Messiah would be the antithesis of Ahaz: the ideal Judge, Statesman, and King.

The "Book of Immanuel" tells of imminent judgment on Israel and Assyria and also predicts a still future event when the "remnant that is left of his people from Assyria, from Lower Egypt, from Upper Egypt, from Cush, from Elam, from Babylonia, from Hamath and from the islands of the sea" will be reclaimed (Isaiah 11:11). This is a remarkable instance of prophecy that has been partially fulfilled, but will not be completely fulfilled until the return of our Lord and the millennium (11:1-16).

Nebuchadnezzar first invaded Judah in 735 B.C. and the first step of the exile began in 605 B.C., 130 years later.

When Isaiah, in response to Ahaz's stupid decision, wrote the "Book of Immanuel," both Israel and Judah still occupied their own territories. Neither the Assyrian nor the Babylonian captivities had begun. Nevertheless Isaiah boldly proclaimed that God's people would return to the land after being scattered all over the earth: "He will assemble the scattered people of Judah from the four quarters of the earth" (Isaiah 11:12). Isaiah clearly indicated that the initial return would not be universal; only a remnant would return: "A remnant will return, a remnant of Jacob will return to the Mighty God. Though your people, O Israel, be like the sand by the sea, only a remnant will return" (Isaiah 10:21-22).

When Isaiah confronted Ahaz, the prophet brought his son Shear-Jashub with him. *Shear-Jashub* means "a remnant will return." It was well over a century later when the captives of Judah were deported to Babylon that the symbolism of the name became prophetic.

Isaiah's prophecy to Ahaz foretold the exile by inference. But when Isaiah dealt with Ahaz's son Hezekiah, the prophet spoke of the exile to Babylon in a clear manner. Hezekiah was a good king, but he was somewhat like Peter in the New Testament. His life was a mixture of faith and impatience. Much of Isaiah's ministry consisted of warning the well-intentioned Hezekiah not to make impetuous international alliances of intrigue against Assyria (see Isaiah 20). His father Ahaz had rejected Isaiah's counsel, but Hezekiah obeyed, and Jerusalem was miraculously delivered (see Isaiah 36–37). Hezekiah's actions at this time were noble. He in effect acknowledged that it was God's Word against Sennacherib's threatening word. And God's Word prevailed:

> The angel of the Lord went out and put to death a hundred and eighty-five thousand men in the Assyrian camp. When the people got up the next morning—there were all the dead bodies! So Sennacherib king of Assyria broke camp and

withdrew. He returned to Nineveh and stayed there
(Isaiah 37:36-37).

This began Assyria's decline. The neo-Babylonian empire was on the ascendancy. At this time Hezekiah did
not seek counsel from Isaiah. He received envoys and
gifts from the king of Babylon and blatantly displayed all
of his treasures.

> There was nothing in his palace or in all his
> kingdom that Hezekiah did not show them.
> Then Isaiah the prophet went to King Hezekiah
> and asked, "What did those men say, and where did
> they come from?"
> "From a distant land," Hezekiah replied. "They
> came to me from Babylon."
> The prophet asked, "What did they see in your
> palace?"
> "They saw everything in my palace," Hezekiah
> said. "There is nothing among my treasures that I
> did not show them."
> Then Isaiah said to Hezekiah, "Hear the word of
> the Lord Almighty: *The time will surely come when
> everything in your palace, and all that your fathers have
> stored up until this day, will be carried off to Babylon.
> Nothing will be left, says the Lord. And some of your
> descendants, your own flesh and blood who will be born to
> you, will be taken away, and they will become eunuchs in
> the palace of the king of Babylon"* (Isaiah 39:2-7, italics
> added).

One hundred thirty years later Isaiah's prophecy to
Hezekiah was literally fulfilled:

> He brought up against them the king of the
> Babylonians, who killed their young men with the
> sword in the sanctuary, and spared neither young
> man nor young woman, old man or aged. God
> handed all of them over to Nebuchadnezzar. He

carried to Babylon all the articles from the temple of God, both large and small, and the treasures of the Lord's temple *and the treasures of the king and his officials* (2 Chronicles 36:17-18, italics added).

When Hezekiah proudly displayed his treasures to the envoys from Babylon, they undoubtedly made a full and complete report, which Nebuchadnezzar used when he later despoiled the temple and robbed the treasures. However there was one treasure he left for the sons and daughters of Judah as they were exiled to Babylon, one that contained far greater riches than the wealth of Babylon: the written Word of God, the Scriptures.

Among the Scriptures was the prophecy by Isaiah, who had foretold not only the exile, but also the return. Isaiah 40–66 exults in the truth that God is still fulfilling the Abrahamic covenant and that there will be a return. In 41:8-10 God says:

> O Israel, my servant, Jacob, whom I have chosen, you descendants of Abraham my friend, I took you from the ends of the earth, from its farthest corners I called you. I said, "You are my servant"; I have chosen you and have not rejected you. So do not fear, for I am with you; do not be dismayed, for I am your God. I will strengthen you and help you; I will uphold you with my righteous right hand.

Isaiah gave many details of events that would accompany the restoration of Jerusalem and the return from exile:

> This is what the Lord says....I am the Lord...who carries out the words of his servants and fulfills the predictions of his messengers, who says of Jerusalem, "It shall be inhabited," of the towns of Judah, "They shall be built," and of their ruins, "I will restore them," who says to the watery deep, "Be dry, and I will dry up your streams," who says of Cyrus, "He is

my shepherd and will accomplish all that I please; he will say of Jerusalem, 'Let it be rebuilt,' and of the temple, 'Let its foundations be laid.'" This is what the Lord says to his anointed, to Cyrus, whose right hand I take hold of to subdue nations before him and to strip kings of their armor, to open doors before him so that gates will not be shut" (Isaiah 44:24,26–45:1).

Isaiah referred to Cyrus as "shepherd" and "anointed" and prophesied that he would be the one to order the rebuilding of Jerusalem and the temple. One hundred years before the fact, the prophet gave the name of the man who would be the king of a different nation. How minutely God literally fulfilled the predictions of Isaiah about the exile!

Such prophecies are not considered possible by those who deny the supernatural content of the Scriptures. Citing these verses in Isaiah 44–45, many scholars attack the historical trustworthiness of the claim that Isaiah wrote the entire book of Isaiah. But one who trusts in the Lord Jesus should have no difficulty believing that the Holy Spirit could predict by name the person and ministry of any man.

The fulfillment of Isaiah 44:27 and 45:1b gives additional evidence of the trustworthiness of the prophetic Scriptures. Frederick A. Tatford in his commentary on Daniel gave this incredible account of the destruction of Babylon:

> The city was divided in two by the river Euphrates, and [says W. Smith] "the river was enclosed on both banks by quays, which were likewise protected by walls and brass gates." (See Jer. 50:15; 51:53,58)....
>   Such a city might well have been deemed impregnable, and Cyrus took the only line of action open to him and, as foretold in Jer. 50:38, diverted the course of the Euphrates into a new channel (as he had previously done with the river Gyndes). He

waited until the supreme religious festival in honour of the god Bel-Marduk and the goddess Ishta, when religious frenzy and drunken revelry held the city in its grasp. Then, opening the new channel, he drew off the waters and, under the guidance of two Babylonian deserters, whom Xenophon calls Gadatas and Gobryas, the Persians made their way up the dry bed of the river, through the two-leaved gates of brass which opened upon it, and into the city itself—precisely as foretold by the prophet Isaiah long before (Isa. 44:27 to 45:2).[1]

The prophecy of Isaiah was a treasure that Nebuchadnezzar did not destroy. It was one of the books that comforted the exiles in Babylon. These Scriptures motivated the Israelites to be faithful to God and they returned to their land a different people.

JEREMIAH

Jeremiah was the most important prophet of the exile. He foretold the exile and lived to see much of his prophecy fulfilled. We know more about the personal life and emotions of Jeremiah than we know about any other prophet.

Jeremiah is a great example of what a prophet is. His call, his proclamation of the word of the Lord, his well-defined distinction between the true and false prophet, the authority with which he thundered God's truth, and the courage with which he faced the agonizing dilemmas of the historical situation help us understand the meaning of the word *prophet*.

He was a man of marked contrasts. By nature he was tender and gentle, but he excoriated the sins of kings and common people alike. He rejoiced when God spoke to him (Jeremiah 15:16), but God's words were often a source of "pain unending" (15:18). He thundered forth God's judgment, yet spoke eloquently of God's love and consolation in chapters 31 and 33.

What a preacher Jeremiah was! Alexander Whyte characterized him as follows:

> We see with what a fiery sensibility he both prepares and delivers his sermons. At one time we hear him groaning over his text as he stands beside the potter at his wheel, while the potter mars his vessel and casts it away. At another time he does not preach for many weeks. He is away at the Euphrates learning how to illustrate and enforce his next sermon, and he preaches it over and over to himself as he sees in the sand the footprints of his captive people.
>
> Another Sabbath morning he takes his elders out to the valley beyond the city, and dashes an earthen vessel to pieces before their amazed and angry eyes, and that is all the sermon they get that morning. A preacher—like a great preacher of our own land—to "terrify even the godly."[2]

Jeremiah's ministry came to a climax during the reign of Zedekiah, Judah's last king. He was a puppet king appointed by Nebuchadnezzar, but Zedekiah loved power and rebelled against Babylon. Nebuchadnezzar was furious and resolved to settle the Jewish problem once and for all. One would naturally think that if Jeremiah were a true prophet, he would pronounce judgment on Babylon, but he did not! He said to the envoys sent by other vassal states to meet with Zedekiah:

> The God of Israel, says: "Tell this to your masters: With my great power and outstretched arm I made the earth and its people and the animals that are on it, and I give it to anyone I please. Now I will hand all your countries over to my servant Nebuchadnezzar king of Babylon; I will make even the wild animals subject to him. All nations will serve him and his son and his grandson until the time for his land comes; then many nations and great kings will subjugate him.

"If, however, any nation or kingdom will not serve Nebuchadnezzar king of Babylon or bow its neck under his yoke, I will punish that nation with the sword, famine and plague, declares the Lord, until I destroy it by his hand. So do not listen to your prophets, your diviners, your interpreters of dreams, your mediums or your sorcerers who tell you, 'You will not serve the king of Babylon.' They prophesy lies to you that will only serve to remove you far from your lands; I will banish you and you will perish. But if any nation will bow its neck under the yoke of the king of Babylon and serve him, I will let that nation remain in its own land to till it and to live there, declares the Lord" (Jeremiah 27:4-11).

Jeremiah was not a traitor; he was a true patriot. He alone realized that the reformation under Josiah was not enough. The prophet's heart burned within him as he observed the moral depravity and the political folly of both the leaders and the people.

The Lord told Jeremiah: "Go up and down the streets of Jerusalem, look around and consider, search through her squares. If you can find but one person who deals honestly and seeks the truth, I will forgive this city" (Jeremiah 5:1). But there was none! Sin abounded everywhere; illicit sex was rampant. The Lord declared: "They are well-fed, lusty stallions, each neighing for another man's wife. Should I not punish them for this?" (5:8-9)

When Nebuchadnezzar first laid siege to Jerusalem, the rich men released their Hebrew slaves; but when the siege was lifted and imminent danger seemed over, the wealthy once more captured their slaves and returned them to bondage. The Lord was displeased:

This is what the Lord, the God of Israel, says: I made a covenant with your forefathers when I brought them out of Egypt, out of the land of slavery. I said, "Every seventh year each of you must free any fellow

Hebrew who has sold himself to you. After he has
served you six years, you must let him go free." Your
fathers, however, did not listen to me or pay attention to me. Recently you repented and did what is
right in my sight: Each of you proclaimed freedom
to his countrymen. You even made a covenant
before me in the house that bears my Name. But
now you have turned around and profaned my
name; each of you has taken back the male and
female slaves you had set free to go where they
wished. You have forced them to become your slaves
again.

Therefore, this is what the Lord says: You have
not obeyed me; you have not proclaimed freedom
for your fellow countrymen. So I now proclaim
"freedom" for you, declares the Lord—"freedom"
to fall by the sword, plague and famine (Jeremiah
34:13-17).

There can be no doubt that the imminent slavery of
the Jews to Babylon was God's hand laid upon the Jewish
nation in punishment for their sins. But he who sees only
this fact misses the grand truth the prophet proclaimed.
God's hand in judgment was to become His arm of love
extended to all men everywhere.

Under the law of Moses it was possible for a Jew to sell
himself into slavery in order to repay a debt. If he did,
God provided the *goel,* the "kinsman-redeemer," whose
main function was to redeem (literally, to buy back) his
brother from his slavery. The law clearly stated:

If an alien or a temporary resident among you
becomes rich and one of your countrymen becomes
poor and sells himself to the alien living among you
or to a member of the alien's clan, he retains the
right of redemption after he has sold himself. One
of his relatives may redeem him. An uncle or a
cousin or any blood relative in his clan may redeem
him (Leviticus 25:47-49).

A *goel* could also redeem his kinsman's possessions. And whenever a Jew's relative was murdered, the kinsman-redeemer became the *goel ha dam*, the "avenger of the blood."

In her wickedness Judah made light of God's provision for redemption. God punished her, but in the midst of her chastening, He Himself became her Redeemer! "Hear the word of the Lord, O nations; proclaim it in distant coastlands: 'He who scattered Israel will gather them and will watch over his flock like a shepherd.' For the Lord will ransom Jacob and redeem them from the hand of those stronger than they" (Jeremiah 31:10-11).

The Encyclopedia of the Jewish Religion describes redemption as follows:

> The religious and theological meanings of redemption are derived from ancient Israelite law and social custom. To "redeem" meant to fulfill the duty of next of kin ("redeemer") by ransoming a kinsman who had sold himself into slavery, or by exercising the option to buy back family property that had been alienated. The next of kin who acts as BLOOD AVENGER is also called *goel*. To describe God as *goel* (cf. Job 19:25, "I know that my Redeemer liveth") is to imply that He is, as it were, the closest and nearest relative. In saving His people (cf. Isa. 11:11; Jer. 31:10), He acts the part of the kinsman in ancient law.[3]

During his lifetime it seemed as if Jeremiah were a failure. After his death, however, his message, his life, and his character had such far-reaching significance that he is rightly considered to be one of the greatest prophets. Six centuries after the exile Matthew wrote: "When Jesus came to the region of Caesarea Philippi, he asked his disciples, 'Who do people say the Son of Man is?' They replied, 'Some say John the Baptist; others say Elijah; and still others, Jeremiah'" (Matthew 16:13-14).

Jeremiah's writings were copied by the scribes during

the seventy years of exile. His message, thus passed on, helped to change the Jewish captives. When a remnant returned and rebuilt Jerusalem and the temple, they were a different people. They were not and still are not idolaters.

THE LAMENTATIONS OF JEREMIAH

The Lamentations of Jeremiah, the most eloquent book in the Bible, is the anguished sob of Jeremiah over the fall of Jerusalem. Time after time Jeremiah had prophesied its destruction and the exile to Babylon, and like our Lord he wept over the city.

All during his long ministry Jeremiah was accused of being a false prophet on the grounds that God would never forsake Jerusalem or let His temple be destroyed. Because he warned about the destruction of the city and the temple, Jeremiah was arrested and placed in stocks. Another time he was lowered by ropes into a dungeon that was filled with mire. However, Jeremiah lived to see that day of judgment and was proved to be a true prophet.

Not many prophets live to see the fulfillment of what they have predicted and a lesser prophet would have gloried in his personal triumph. But not Jeremiah! His anguish over the destruction was unbearable even though he had known it would happen. He lamented: "How deserted lies the city, once so full of people! How like a widow is she, who once was great among the nations! She who was queen among the provinces has now become a slave" (Lamentations 1:1). In grief anticipatory of our Lord, Jeremiah wept: "Is it nothing to you, all you who pass by? Look around and see. Is any suffering like my suffering that was inflicted on me, that the Lord brought on me in the day of his fierce anger?" (1:12).

Because the book of Lamentations is poetry, it has been neglected by some as source material in the study of the history of Judah. However, the book is the only extant eyewitness account of the destruction of Jerusalem.

Before reading Lamentations, carefully study the

curses for disobedience that were prophesied by Moses in Deuteronomy 28:15-68 and note how the prophecy of Moses was fulfilled as described in Lamentations. Deuteronomy 28:53-55, for example, foretold the horrors of starvation that would befall Jerusalem:

> Because of the suffering that your enemy will inflict on you during the siege, you will eat the fruit of the womb, the flesh of the sons and daughters the Lord your God has given you. Even the most gentle and sensitive man among you will have no compassion on his own brother or the wife he loves or his surviving children, and he will not give to one of them any of the flesh of his children that he is eating.

Nine centuries later Jeremiah lamented over the fulfillment of this terrifying prophecy of Moses:

> Those killed by the sword are better off than those who die of famine; racked with hunger, they waste away for lack of food from the field. With their own hands compassionate women have cooked their own children, who became their food when my people were destroyed (Lamentations 4:9-10).

If it were not for Lamentations, we would never know how literally the prophecies of Moses were fulfilled during the destruction of Jerusalem by Nebuchadnezzar.

The first four chapters of Lamentations are poems that are also acrostics. In chapters 1, 2, and 4 the verses begin with successive letters of the Hebrew alphabet. For example verse 1 begins with the letter *aleph*; verse 2, *beth*; and so forth. Chapter 3 is a triple acrostic. Each stanza has three verses. The verses of each stanza begin with successive letters of the Hebrew alphabet. (*The New Scofield Bible* tells us that "the fifth chapter, although not alphabetical, contains twenty-two verses in a plaintive meter, which—the second half of each verse being

shorter than the first—conveys a somber effect of diminu-
endo."[4]) The rabbis say that these acrostics express
Israel's suffering from *aleph* to *tau*—that is, from A to Z.

An acrostic is an aid to memory. Lamentations was written to be memorized. There are other acrostics in the
Scriptures, Psalm 119 being the best known. Each of its
stanzas has eight verses, all of which begin with the same
letter of the alphabet.

Each year on the ninth day of Av (usually in August)
the Jews keep a solemn fast commemorating the destruction of Solomon's temple, over which Jeremiah so deeply
lamented. The oldest member of the congregation an-
nounces, "This is the ——th year since the destruction
of the holy temple." He then exhorts the congregation
as follows: "Each generation in which the temple is not
rebuilt should regard itself as responsible for its destruction." Later the entire book of Lamentations is recited
from memory in dim candlelight while the congregation
sits on the floor.

Many other terrible events of Jewish history occurred
on the ninth day of Av and are also commemorated on
this day. The *Encyclopedia Judaica* states:

> The Mishnah (Ta'an 4:6) enumerates five disasters:
> (1) On the 9th of Av it was decreed that the Children
> of Israel, after the Exodus from Egypt, should not
> enter the Promised Land; (2) the First and (3) the
> Second Temples were destroyed; (4) Bethar, the last
> stronghold of the leaders of the Bar Kokhba war,
> was captured in 135 c.e.;[5] and (5) one year later, in
> 136, the Roman emperor Hadrian established a
> heathen temple on the site of the Temple and
> rebuilt Jerusalem as a pagan city which was renamed
> *Aelia Capitolina* and which the Jews were forbidden
> to enter.
> The expulsion of the Jews from Spain in 1492 is
> said also to have occurred on the 9th of Av.
> The 9th of Av thus became a symbol for all the
> persecutions and misfortunes of the Jewish people,

for the loss of national independence and the sufferings in exile.[6]

Since the book of Lamentations is essentially poetry, it is difficult to identify a particular theme in the individual chapters. However, certain subjects do stand out in each poem:

Chapter 1   repeats Jerusalem's distress because its people are abandoned by their former allies.

Chapter 2   expresses God's role in Jerusalem's destruction. The Lord is the executor of judgment.

Chapter 3   describes the meaning of suffering.

Chapter 4   stresses the inhabitants' sufferings.

Chapter 5   is a prayer of hope.

The core of the book of Lamentations is found in chapter 3, where Jeremiah expressed the meaning of suffering. In verses 1-21 he described his own peculiar sufferings during those days. Observe that he used the first person time and time again: "*I* am," "He has driven *me*," "He pierced *my* heart" (italics added).

Later in verses 25-66 he used the third person: "*Those* whose hope is in him," "pursue *them*" (italics added). In other words, Jeremiah described his suffering as caused not so much by his own sins as by the unrighteousness of his people. The latter part of chapter 3 is a psalm of repentance—not Jeremiah's, but the people's.

In between the "I" of the first verses and the "they" of the latter verses is expressed one of the most overwhelming truths of the Scriptures: "Because of the Lord's great love we are not consumed, for his compassions never fail. They are new every morning; great is your faithfulness" (3:22-23). *Compassion* is "the act of suffering together." In the depths of his suffering Jeremiah realized that he did not suffer alone. God suffered with Jeremiah and He suffered with His people.

The book of Lamentations is an answer to one of mankind's most troubling questions: Why do people suffer?

There is no easy answer. In Lamentations, as far as Judah is concerned, the answer is sin: "Why should any living man complain when punished for his sins?" (3:39)

But why do the righteous suffer? Why should Jeremiah have suffered when throughout his whole life he waged war against sin? Jeremiah sublimated this seemingly unanswerable question to a deeper truth: Not only did Jeremiah suffer; God also suffered. He suffered with Jeremiah and His people just as He suffers with all men today. This is the compassion of God!

EZEKIEL

Ezekiel is the most neglected prophet in the Bible. One of the reasons for this neglect is the fact that he frequently spoke of visions and symbols that are not easy to interpret. We should realize that these conceptions are part of God's revelation. Their purpose is to reveal, not to conceal.

In the Old Testament Scriptures all prophets, whether they were empowered to predict the future or anointed to proclaim God's message, spoke to a historical situation. Ezekiel 1:2-3 is the key to the circumstances that confronted Ezekiel: "It was the fifth year of the exile of King Jehoiachin—the word of the Lord came to Ezekiel the priest, the son of Buzi, by the Kebar River in the land of the Babylonians. There the hand of the Lord was upon him." At this time the exile was partial. Only the elite of Jerusalem had been carried away. The young priest Ezekiel was among the leading men of the land who were exiled. Second Kings 24:13-16 provides additional information about the times:

> As the Lord had declared, Nebuchadnezzar removed all the treasures from the temple of the Lord and from the royal palace, and took away all the gold articles that Solomon king of Israel had made for the temple of the Lord. He carried into exile all Jerusalem: all the officers and fighting men, and all

the craftsmen and artisans—a total of ten thousand. Only the poorest people of the land were left.

Nebuchadnezzar took Jehoiachin captive to Babylon. He also took from Jerusalem to Babylon the king's mother, his wives, his officials and the leading men of the land. The king of Babylon also deported to Babylon the entire force of seven thousand fighting men, strong and fit for war, and a thousand craftsmen and artisans.

When Nebuchadnezzar first conquered Jerusalem, he did not destroy the city or the temple. The Jewish state was still in existence. A king was even allowed to rule the city and as long as he remained loyal to Babylon, he was left in peace. Even more important, the temple was still standing. The false prophets who had harassed Jeremiah were still active. They continued to spread the propaganda that the existence of the temple, which was the dwelling place of God, was a guarantee that the exile would be short-lived.

The exiles became obsessed with the irrational idea that Babylon would soon be defeated and that they would then be free to return. It was Ezekiel's painful task to predict the complete fall of Jerusalem and the destruction of the temple. This is the burden of the first division (chapters 1–24) of the book of Ezekiel.

The name *Ezekiel* means "strengthened by God." Ezekiel received God's strength at his commission (see Ezekiel 1–2). Like Moses, Isaiah, and the apostle John, Ezekiel received a special revelation of God's power and majesty. But Ezekiel's vision was unique: he saw "an immense cloud with flashing lightning and surrounded by brilliant light," a chariot "like glowing metal," and in the fire "what looked like four living creatures" (1:4-5). These creatures were undoubtedly the cherubim, the celestial beings who guard the tree of life east of the garden of Eden (see Genesis 3:24).

The most important element in Ezekiel's vision was "a figure like that of a man" (Ezekiel 1:26). "Like the appearance of a rainbow in the clouds on a rainy day, so was the radiance around him. This was the appearance of the likeness of the glory of the Lord" (1:28).

Ezekiel's vision of the holiness and power of God encompassed the entire prophecy concerning the earth (the Jews in Israel, the Jews in Babylon, the Babylonians, the warring nations of the world) and above the earth (the glory of the Lord). Ezekiel saw that *God is in complete control of history.* He was at work even in the exile, which seemed to be a most disastrous calamity. He was—and still is—remembering His promise to Abraham: "All peoples on earth will be blessed through you" (Genesis 12:3). Charles R. Eerdman wrote: "Such a symbolic vision of the power and holiness of God is a fitting preface to the Book of Ezekiel. His prophecies form a unique collection of pictures, of images, of parables and of dreams. He is the supreme mystic among the inspired writers."[7]

Ezekiel began his prophesying with predictions of dire judgment. Some of his prophecies were expressed in a series of symbolic acts: he made a map of Jerusalem under siege (Ezekiel 4:1); he ate food cooked over manure (4:15), thus foretelling the coming famine; he shaved his head and burned his hair (5:1-4), indicating that a fire would spread to the whole house of Israel. Ezekiel also made direct prophecies of the siege, the famine and pestilence, and the destruction of Jerusalem.

As he made his horrible prophecies, Ezekiel developed an important truth: the moral responsibility of the individual. The righteous remnant in Israel bitterly complained that they were being punished for the sins of their ancestors. They murmured, "The fathers eat sour grapes, and the children's teeth are set on edge" (Ezekiel 18:2). They believed the exile was merely corporate judgment and they did not deserve it. Ezekiel set them straight: "The soul who sins is the one who will die" (18:4). Roland K. Harrison wrote:

> The great contribution of the prophet Ezekiel
> to the doctrine of man lies in his emphasis upon

personal responsibility. The New Covenant (Jer. 31:31ff; cf. Ezek. 36:26ff) would not exhibit a corporate character in the strictly Mosaic sense, but would be made with a redeemed society formulated on the basis of individuals who responded to the free expression of divine love. Because everything in the future was to be based upon divine grace, the relationship of the individual to God was not dependent upon considerations of heredity and environment, any more than it was on past religious and historical influences (Ezek. 18:1ff; 33:10ff).[8]

As we continue in this first section of Ezekiel (chapters 1–24), we notice that the tone becomes darker and drearier. Ezekiel saw the literal fulfillment of his prophecies of the destruction of Jerusalem. On the exact date that Nebuchadnezzar laid siege to Jerusalem, Ezekiel's wife died and God forbade Ezekiel to mourn (Ezekiel 24:15-17). He hid his grief and on the day following her death he went on as usual (24:18).

The people in exile in Babylon would soon learn that Jerusalem had fallen and that it was too late to repent. They were not to mourn over the city and the temple, which were as dear to them as a wife is to her husband. The exiles too were to bow in silence in the face of their beloved city's destruction. It was part of God's judgment.

While the first section of Ezekiel denounces Israel and predicts the fall of Jerusalem, the second section (chapters 25–32) deals with the nations surrounding Israel. These cruel neighbors rejoiced over the fall of Jerusalem, but Ezekiel pronounced their doom.

God is no respecter of persons or nations. He had punished Israel for its sins and was not going to permit its pagan enemies to escape His hand of judgment: "There will be trouble and distress for every human being who does evil: first for the Jew, then for the Gentile" (Romans 2:9). The book of Ezekiel, which is a remarkable witness to the accuracy of predictive prophecy, proves that even though the Jews are in the hands of the nations, the nations themselves are in the hands of God.

The third section of Ezekiel (chapters 33–48) describes the holiness of the God who would restore all things. When the news of Jerusalem's fall finally reached Babylon (Ezekiel 33:21) and the exiles were horrified and despondent, the prophecies of Ezekiel changed. Before this he was a prophet of doom and judgment; from this time on he became a prophet of joy and hope. Earlier he proclaimed that because God is holy, He would destroy Jerusalem. Now he argued that the same truth— the holiness of God—would make the ultimate restoration of Israel necessary. God would keep His word:

> This is what the Sovereign Lord says: It is not for your sake, O house of Israel, that I am going to do these things, but for the sake of my holy name, which you have profaned among the nations....
>
> For I will take you out of the nations; I will gather you from all the countries and bring you back into your own land (Ezekiel 36:22,24).

This restoration will be to a redeemed people: "On the day I cleanse you from all your sins, I will resettle your towns" (36:33).

Included in this third section of Ezekiel is the marvelous vision of the valley of dry bones (37:1-14). This passage proclaims the resurrection of the nation: "I am going to open your graves and bring you up from them; I will bring you back to the land of Israel" (37:12).

Ezekiel predicted a new Jerusalem, a redeemed people, and a rebuilt temple (chapters 40–48), which would become the center of Israel's national life. Shortly before the fall of Jerusalem, Ezekiel had watched as the "glory of the Lord departed from over the threshold of the temple" (Ezekiel 10:18). After the fall of Jerusalem, he wrote: "I saw the glory of the God of Israel coming from the east....He said: 'Son of man, this is the place of my throne and the place for the soles of my feet. This is where I will live among the Israelites forever'" (43:2,7).

Ezekiel's vision was of a holy nation worshiping a holy God in a redeemed Jerusalem, in the midst of which was the rebuilt temple. That temple will be the dwelling place of God and from it will flow the river of God, which will be for the healing of the nations (Ezekiel 47:1-12). "And the name of the city from that time on will be: The Lord Is There" (48:35).

DANIEL

Daniel, the most successful prophet in the Scriptures, was among the first group of exiles. These included "some of the Israelites from the royal family and the nobility—young men without any physical defect, handsome, showing aptitude for every kind of learning, well informed, quick to understand, and qualified to serve in the king's palace." These young men were to be taught "the language and literature of the Babylonians" and fed "a daily amount of food and wine from the king's table. They were to be trained for three years, and after that they were to enter the king's service" (Daniel 1:3-5).

Four of these Jewish princes and nobles—Daniel, Shadrach, Meshach, and Abednego—fearful that they would be defiled by eating ceremonially unclean food, asked for and received permission to eat only plain vegetables and drink only water. In spite of their simple diet, the four friends showed perfect body development. They studied diligently and God rewarded their faithful study with intelligence that was "ten times better than all the magicians and enchanters" in Babylon (Daniel 1:20)!

Daniel, through the power of God, was able to interpret the king's dream of the gold-silver-iron-clay image. The king rewarded him by making him governor of the province of Babylon and giving his three friends executive positions. In spite of their high posts, the four friends remained loyal to God.

Then Nebuchadnezzar set up a gold image as a symbol of his power. Shadrach, Meshach, and Abednego refused to worship this image and as a result were thrown into the blazing furnace. But in the midst of the flames there appeared One like the Son of God and He preserved them. Nebuchadnezzar was impressed by this miracle and commanded that all of his subjects respect the God of the Jews (Daniel 3:1-30).

Later, in the reign of Belshazzar, Daniel was called in to interpret the mysterious handwriting that appeared on the walls of the palace during the king's blasphemous feast. The interpretation given by Daniel was that Babylon would immediately be conquered by the Persians.

After this prophecy was fulfilled, Darius the Mede made Daniel one of three administrators over all of Persia's satraps. His fellow rulers were intensely jealous of the favors that were bestowed on him. They flattered the king into issuing a decree that forbade all prayers except those offered to the king himself for a period of thirty days. Daniel remained faithful to God and broke the law, so Darius had to carry out the prescribed penalty. He cast his conscientious administrator into a den of lions. But God preserved Daniel, and his persecutors suffered the fate that they had intended for the prophet.

Arno C. Gaebelein wrote:

> We know more of the personal history of Daniel, of his character, than of any of the other Prophets. What a man of faith he was! In the great Faith chapter of the New Testament, in the cloud of witnesses, his name is not mentioned, but his deeds are there. "Who through faith subdued kingdoms, wrought righteousness, obtained promises, stopped the mouths of lions" (Hebrews xi. 33). Who is able to describe this truly great man? As a mere lad he was brought from Jerusalem to Babylon. In a short time he rose to the highest position in the empire. He continued even unto the first year of King Cyrus. What faithfulness is exhibited in his life. His

dependence on God, his deep piety and humility are mentioned in nearly every chapter of the Book. He was a great man of prayer. He talked with angels and the angel Gabriel addressed him thrice as "the man greatly beloved." The Lord appeared unto him and he had the visions of God. He outlived the captivity of seventy years and was a very old man when Jehovah, whom he knew so well and whom he had so greatly honored by his faith, gave him the promise. "But go thy way till the end be; for thou shalt rest, and stand in thy lot at the end of the days" (Chapter xii. 13).[9]

But the main purpose of the book of Daniel is not to give his biography. It includes only a few events of his long career. It does not give his lineage or his age. Neither does it give us a record of the history of Israel during the exile. The purpose of the book of Daniel is to comfort and assure the people of God that even though God exiled them because of their sins, the exile did not annul God's covenant with Abraham.

When the Jews were exiled to Babylon, the "times of the Gentiles" began. The Jews were in the hands of the nations. But Daniel's message is that these nations themselves are in the hands of God! Babylon, which conquered Israel, would in Daniel's lifetime be conquered by Medo-Persia. Persia, in turn, would be conquered by Greece, and Greece by Rome. But "in the time of those kings, the God of heaven will set up a kingdom that will never be destroyed, nor will it be left to another people. It will crush all those kingdoms and bring them to an end, but it will itself endure forever" (Daniel 2:44).

Daniel, who was exiled to Babylon, prophesied the same truth that John, who was exiled on the isle of Patmos, later foretold: "The kingdom of the world has become the kingdom of our Lord and of his Christ, and he will reign for ever and ever" (Revelation 11:15). This quotation from the book of Revelation illustrates another truth: if we did not have the prophecy of Daniel, Revelation would be a sealed book. The converse is also true: without Revelation we would not understand Daniel. The book of Daniel is the indispensable introduction to New Testament prophecy.

2
The Jews in Babylon

B y the rivers of Babylon we sat and wept" (Psalm 137:1). The rivers of Babylon were the Tigris and the Euphrates, which were two of the four head-streams that watered the garden of Eden (see Genesis 2:14). To many of the exiles, Babylon was a garden of Eden. Solomon Grayzel explained:

> Babylonia presented a contrast to Judea, and Babylon to Jerusalem. The lofty walls of Babylon, the towering domes of its temples, its hanging gardens, its massive palaces, made the Jews think of Jerusalem as small-townish. How could the Temple, even with the solemnity of its service, compare to the stateliness of the sacrificial rites of the temples of Marduk or Ishtar, chief gods of Babylon, or the simple vestments of Jerusalem's priests with the gorgeous garments of the priests of Babylon?
>
> On the streets of this conquering city, mistress of the world, men from every nation, every race and color, could be seen. In its market-stalls wares, imported from remote peoples whose very names were unpronounceable, could be admired and purchased. Its book-stalls, conducted by men known as public scribes, contained a varied banquet of wisdom and entertainment.

Through this magnificent and proud city, the Judean exile walked. He was overwhelmed by it. He might hate it at first for having brought misfortune upon him and his people. But as time went on and his personal life became easier, he was inclined to admit that there was no use struggling against anything so powerful and dazzling as Babylonian civilization. He might even be overheard admitting to his friends that, while he himself could never forget he was a Judean, it might be just as well for his children to grow up citizens of mighty Babylonia.[1]

The fact that the temple was destroyed and the Judeans themselves were now exiles seemed to these people proof that Jehovah was impotent. Many of them abandoned their faith and conveniently adopted the religion of their conquerors. They, like the ten tribes of Israel, have disappeared from history.

But there continued to be a remnant! Isaiah had prophesied almost two centuries before the destruction of the temple that "in that day the remnant of Israel, the survivors of the house of Jacob, will no longer rely on him who struck them down but will truly rely on the Lord, the Holy One of Israel. A remnant will return, a remnant of Jacob will return to the Mighty God" (Isaiah 10:20-21).

Bible scholars use the term *redemption history* in reference to the history recorded in the Bible. From the time of the Babylonian captivity on, redemption history became the story of this Jewish remnant.

God even used Nebuchadnezzar in redemption history. He was a cruel conqueror, but he was not a cruel master. His captives were not slaves. They were settled in various parts of his kingdom. Although they could not return to Jerusalem, they could receive mail from those left behind. Jeremiah wrote "from Jerusalem to the surviving elders among the exiles and to the priests, the prophets and all the other people":

This is what the Lord Almighty, the God of Israel, says to all those I carried into exile from Jerusalem to Babylon: "Build houses and settle down; plant gardens and eat what they produce. Marry and have sons and daughters; find wives for your sons and give your daughters in marriage, so that they too may have sons and daughters....When seventy years are completed for Babylon, I will come to you and fulfill my gracious promise to bring you back to this place. For I know the plans I have for you...plans to prosper you and not to harm you, plans to give you hope and a future...I will gather you from all the nations and places where I have banished you...and will bring you back to the place from which I carried you into exile" (Jeremiah 29:1,4-6,10-11,14).

From the letter of Jeremiah we are able to glean several facts about the remnant of the Jews in Babylon:

1. The elders of the Jews continued their office.
2. The priests and the prophets still ministered.
3. The Jews were permitted to build houses.
4. Their family life remained intact.
5. They believed that they would return after seventy years.

The remnant realized that the exile was a punishment for their unfaithfulness to the God of Israel. Idolatry had been rampant among the Jews before the exile, but when the remnant returned seventy years later, they were a transformed people. No longer would they follow their leaders into idol worship.

Although the Jews in Babylon could no longer attend their temple and could no longer sacrifice animals, some still continued to gather to worship Jehovah. We know from Ezekiel 8:1 that the elders worshiped together; the prophet wrote, "While I was sitting in my house and the elders of Judah were sitting before me, the hand of the Sovereign Lord came upon me." Some scholars believe this meeting in Ezekiel's home was the beginning of the synagogue.

In Babylon certain days were observed as rest days (or sabbaths) and therefore it was not difficult for the Jews to keep the sabbath more strictly than they ever had before. They could meet for worship, for the discussion of religious questions, and for the reading of passages from the prophetic and historical books of the Scriptures. Charles F. Pfeiffer wrote:

> In place of the Temple, synagogues became the accepted houses of worship. There the sacred Torah was read and explained. It comprised the first five books of the Bible, the Pentateuch. The word "Torah" is usually translated "law," but might better be rendered "instruction."
>
> The *Torah* gave instruction by example as well as by precept. Ultimately other sacred books were accepted as inspired Scripture. Jeremiah was lightly dismissed during the years of his ministry in Jerusalem, but in Babylonian exile his countrymen came to see that his prophecies were true.
>
> A collection of the "Prophets"—including some of our historical books—came into being. The Synagogue also recognized a third section of the Old Testament, the "Writings," beginning with the Book of Psalms and including books of poetry as well as history and prophecy.
>
> The New Testament bears testimony to the Law, the Prophets, and the Psalms as the three sections of Scripture. This threefold division is still used in printed editions of the Hebrew Bible.[2]

Moreover a body of men called scribes came into being. Originally disciples of priests and prophets, the scribes meticulously made copies of the Law, the Writings, and the Prophets. The most famous scribe of all was Ezra.

During the exile, family registers were carefully kept, the old customs were preserved, and the details of the temple services were minutely recorded in preparation for the time when the Jews would return and resume their life in Jerusalem.

Meanwhile there were tremendous upheavals throughout the world. Judah was not the only nation that resisted Nebuchadnezzar. Another was Tyre, which made an alliance with Egypt. The Babylonians besieged Tyre for thirteen years (see Ezekiel 29:17-21) and finally defeated them, but the bold resistance of the Tyrians encouraged other nations to revolt. (When the Babylonians entered Tyre, they found only an empty shell, for the people had escaped with their wealth!) The siege of Tyre was followed by an attack against Egypt and in 568 B.C. Nebuchadnezzar's armies occupied Egypt's frontier.

In 562 B.C. Nebuchadnezzar died. His kingdom did not survive his death very long, for civil wars broke out and the empire disintegrated. Within six years there were four kings and two revolutions. Meanwhile the exiled Jews read the prophetic Scriptures. They were encouraged by the words of Jeremiah 25:12-14:

> "But when the seventy years are fulfilled, I will punish the king of Babylon and his nation, the land of the Babylonians, for their guilt," declares the Lord, "and will make it desolate forever. I will bring upon that land all the things I have spoken against it, all that are written in this book and prophesied by Jeremiah against all the nations. They themselves will be enslaved by many nations and great kings; I will repay them according to their deeds and the work of their hands."

Judah's remnant waited; they would soon return!

3

The Jewish Nation under Persia

THE FALL OF BABYLON

Nebuchadnezzar ruled in Babylon for forty-four years. He died in 562 B.C. and was succeeded by his son Evil-Merodach, who is mentioned in 2 Kings 25:27-30. From this passage we learn that he liberated Jehoiachin and apparently recognized him as Judah's king.

Evil-Merodach's reign was short—only two years. He was assassinated by his brother-in-law Neriglissar, who also ruled only two years. His son Labashi Mardok had reigned less than a year when Nabinidus usurped his throne. Nabinidus was the father of Belshazzar, whose story is told in Daniel 5:

> King Belshazzar gave a great banquet for a thousand of his nobles and drank wine with them. While Belshazzar was drinking his wine, he gave orders to bring in the gold and silver goblets that Nebuchadnezzar his father [ancestor or predecessor] had taken from the temple in Jerusalem, so that the king and his nobles, his wives and his

concubines might drink from them. So they brought in the gold goblets that had been taken from the temple of God in Jerusalem, and the king and his nobles, his wives and his concubines drank from them. As they drank the wine, they praised the gods of gold and silver, of bronze, iron, wood and stone.

Suddenly the fingers of a human hand appeared and wrote on the plaster of the wall, near the lampstand in the royal palace. The king watched the hand as it wrote. His face turned pale and he was so frightened that his knees knocked together and his legs gave way....

That very night Belshazzar, king of the Babylonians, was slain, and Darius the Mede took over the kingdom (Daniel 5:1-6,30).

It is important to study the story of the temple vessels in the Bible. They are mentioned in the Scriptural accounts of the three occasions when Nebuchadnezzar assaulted Jerusalem (see Daniel 1:1-2 for the first assault; 2 Chronicles 36:10 and Jeremiah 27:16 for the second; and 2 Chronicles 36:18 for the final destruction).

The removing of the temple vessels was not merely an act of looting, for Nebuchadnezzar considered himself to be serving his god Marduk. When Nebuchadnezzar attacked Judah, the battle was not just between Babylon and Judah; to him the battle was between Marduk and Jehovah!

When Nebuchadnezzar defeated an enemy, he not only deported its people; he also "captured" its gods and set them up in "the treasure house of his god" (Daniel 1:2). However when Nebuchadnezzar sacked the temple in Jerusalem, there were no idols to take, so he took the treasures of the Lord's temple with him instead. Since these vessels represented the God of the Jews to the Babylonians, Belshazzar's feast was not a mere orgy; it was a direct challenge to Jehovah. Dr. Charles L. Feinberg explained the outcome as recorded in Daniel 5:30-31:

Verse 30: That same night, so soon after the judgment was pronounced, its provisions were fulfilled. Belshazzar was slain, and the connection between his sin and his fall was inescapable.

Cyrus the Persian showed great military prowess. He diverted the Euphrates River into a new channel and marched his army into Babylon through the dry riverbed while the Babylonians were still carousing.

Verse 31: Although the city was actually taken by Cyrus, it was done in the name of Cyrus's uncle, Darius the Mede. Thus Babylon came to a disgraceful end when it impiously laid its hands on the sacred vessels of God. Remember, God has means of bringing the proudest down to destruction.[1]

The fall of Babylon was sudden, startling, and complete.

THE RISE OF PERSIA UNDER CYRUS

There are few events in history that are as significant as the reign of Cyrus the Great. Yet the facts of his birth are obscure; he just suddenly appeared on the pages of history. However, Isaiah had prophesied of him:

> This is what the Lord says....I am the Lord...who says of Cyrus, "He is my shepherd and will accomplish all that I please; he will say of Jerusalem, 'Let it be rebuilt,' and of the temple, 'Let its foundations be laid.'" This is what the Lord says to his anointed, to Cyrus, whose right hand I take hold of to subdue nations before him and to strip kings of their armor, to open doors before him so that gates will not be shut....I will raise up Cyrus in my righteousness: I will make all his ways straight. He will rebuild my city and set my exiles free (Isaiah 44:24,28; 45:1,13).

In 560 B.C. Cyrus became the king of Anshan, a petty kingdom-state, and soon incorporated the province of Parsua. Ten years later he became king of Media and eleven years after that he conquered Babylon. Before his final battle he transferred his kingdom to his son Cambysses.

The Persian empire then extended from the Mediterranean sea to the Indus river in India. It included twenty satrapies from Israel, Syria, Phoenicia, Lydia, Phrygia, Ionia, Cappadocia, Calicia, Armenia, Assyria, the Caucasus, Babylonia, Media, Persia, modern Afghanistan and Baluchistan, as well as western India. Never before had one government controlled such a wide area! Isaiah had said that Cyrus would subdue nations before him. Max I. Dimont wrote in his excellent history of the Jewish people:

> After four millenniums of Semitic civilizations, Asia Minor fell under the rule of a new people, the Persians, and a new race, the Aryans, late-comers to the circle of culture bearers. In the sixth century B.C., when Babylonia stood at the height of her power, there was no Persia.
>
> Who in 1910 would have believed that England, then the undisputed ruler of the seas, in another fifty years would sink to the status of a third-class power, and that Russia, then a third-class power, in the same time would rise to be a dominant world force?
>
> Who in 600 B.C. would have believed that in another fifty years Babylonia, then the ruler of the world, would be wiped off the face of the earth by a people who did not as yet exist? Yet history had slated this unknown people to become the inheritors of the civilized world.[2]

Cyrus was a different kind of king. Both his political and religious deeds were in contrast to those of all the world rulers who preceded him. Instead of humiliating the people he conquered, he did everything possible to reconcile them. Instead of forcing his new subjects to acknowledge his gods, he encouraged them to continue to worship their gods. In many instances he actually joined his subjects in their worship. F. F. Bruce wrote:

> Cyrus, whose personal religious views are not easy to determine, had no intention of offending his subjects' religious susceptibilities by such a policy; on the contrary, he would conciliate these susceptibilities by playing the part of a worshipper of their various gods. "The Great King," as one scholar has remarked, "had no objection to bowing in the house of Rimmon if there was anything to be picked up on the floor." There is evidence from other parts of the Persian Empire that this policy was not followed in Babylonia only.
>
> Against this background we can appreciate the political motives of Cyrus's action with regard to the Jews. [3]

In the centuries before Cyrus, world rulers used different policies to maintain control of their realms. Assyria had a policy of permanent transportation: they settled their vanquished peoples on the lands of other nations they had conquered. This meant that there was no hope for the ten northern tribes of Israel to return to their homeland and they were assimilated.

The Babylonians also deported conquered peoples. However when the Jews were deported to Babylonia, Nebuchadnezzar did not resettle the land; there were no new owners. This made it possible for the Jews to return.

The policies of the Assyrians and Babylonians filled their empires with multitudes of discontented, rebellious displaced people. They were in a constant state of revolt. The Babylonians could never conquer Egypt because their armies were busy quelling rebellions all over the empire.

When Cyrus conquered a nation, it became a satrapy. He allowed the defeated peoples to worship their gods and to keep their old customs; thus they were more content. However, Cyrus's motives were not humanitarian. He wanted to use the Persian armies for further conquests.

It was easy for Cyrus to win the loyalty of the defeated nations. As his policy became known all over the world, his fame increased. Thus when he entered Babylon, he came not as its conqueror, but as its deliverer. Charles F. Pfeiffer wrote:

> When Cyrus became lord of Babylonia, the dependencies of Babylon likewise came under his control. He adopted a benevolent policy toward those former Babylonian provinces on the principle that the happier their lot, the more likely they would be to co-operate with Persian aims and goals. Phoenicia pledged its loyalty and its fleet, which was the match of any the united Greeks could raise.
>
> The policy of the restoration of captive deities and captive peoples had special application to the Jews, whose religious ideals were respected by Cyrus and his successors as superior to those of the other nations with whom they dealt. To be sure, the Jews had no image that must be restored to its shrine, but Nebuchadnezzar had taken utensils from the Temple at Jerusalem. They had been used in Belshazzar's feast. If the gods of the other nations were restored, certainly the vessels used in the worship of the God of Israel must receive similar treatment.[4]

THE RETURN FROM EXILE

The Decree of Cyrus

The Chronicles are the last books in the Hebrew Bible and they close with the decree of Cyrus. The last verses of 2 Chronicles read:

[Nebuchadnezzar] carried into exile to Babylon the remnant, who escaped from the sword, and they became servants to him and his sons until the kingdom of Persia came to power. The land enjoyed its sabbath rests; all the time of its desolation it rested, until the seventy years were completed in fulfillment of the word of the Lord spoken by Jeremiah.

In the first year of Cyrus king of Persia, in order to fulfill the word of the Lord spoken by Jeremiah, the Lord moved the heart of Cyrus king of Persia to make a proclamation throughout his realm and to put it in writing: "This is what Cyrus king of Persia says: 'The Lord, the God of heaven, has given me all the kingdoms of the earth and he has appointed me to build a temple for him at Jerusalem in Judah. Anyone of his people among you—may the Lord his God be with him, and let him go up'" (36:20-23).

Cyrus, who called himself "the great king," made a proclamation and put it in writing. Centuries earlier a greater King had made another proclamation and put it in writing: "All peoples on earth will be blessed through you" (Genesis 12:3). Cyrus was called "the Great" because the greater One used him to bring the Jews back to their land to fulfill the Abrahamic covenant—to prepare for the coming of the Messiah.

The exodus from Egypt is not the only exodus in the Old Testament; the return of the Jews from Babylon during the reign of Cyrus is another exodus. God's control of history is seen in both. H. L. Ellison wrote:

The story of the Exodus from Egypt is filled with miracles and signs, from the bush that burnt but was not consumed, up to the waters of the Sea of Reeds that flowed back, drowning the pursuing Egyptians. Compared with it, the story of the return from Babylonia seems devoid of any manifestation of Divine action. Yet, when we look at the story more closely, God's mighty hand is seen at every turn. The spiritual baby needs the visibly wonderful at every turn; the mature believer should be able to see the working of God by faith, where the normal person can discern only the working out of natural law.[5]

One of the most amazing evidences of God's control of Jewish history is the edict of Cyrus, king of Persia. Ezra also recorded the decree:

> This is what Cyrus king of Persia says: "The Lord, the God of heaven, has given me all the kingdoms of the earth and he has appointed me to build a temple for him at Jerusalem in Judah. Anyone of his people among you—may his God be with him, and let him go up to Jerusalem in Judah and build the temple of the Lord, the God of Israel, the God who is in Jerusalem. And the people of any place where survivors may now be living are to provide him with silver and gold, with goods and livestock, and with freewill offerings for the temple of God in Jerusalem" (Ezra 1:2-4).

Why would a Zoroastrian king issue such an edict? The hand of God was evident, but Josephus attributed Cyrus's action to his reading of Isaiah 44:28–45:7. Josephus wrote:

> This was known to Cyrus by his reading the book which Isaiah left behind him of his prophecies; for this prophet said that God had spoken thus to him in a secret vision: "My will is, that Cyrus, whom I have appointed to be king over many and great nations, send back my people to their own land, and build my temple."
> This was foretold by Isaiah one hundred and forty years before the temple was demolished. Accordingly, when Cyrus read this, and admired the Divine power, an earnest desire and ambition seized upon him to fulfill what was so written; so he called for

the most eminent Jews that were in Babylon, and
said to them, that he gave them leave to go back to
their own country, and to rebuild their city
Jerusalem, and the temple of God.[6]

Some historians doubt Josephus's explanation. The
Bible simply states, "The Lord moved the heart of Cyrus
king of Persia to make a proclamation" (Ezra 1:1).

Another seemingly incidental detail mentioned earlier proves that God was in control of history: when Nebuchadnezzar destroyed Jerusalem, he did not send in new
settlers to occupy the land. The land remained unplowed.
If another nation had been resettled in Jerusalem, the
return of the Jews would probably have been impossible.

Three great men were the instruments of God in the
return and the rebuilding of the temple: Ezra, Nehemiah,
and Zerubbabel. They stirred up their countrymen to
return to their own land. Because of the enthusiasm and
energetic leadership of these three heroes, the temple
was finally rebuilt and the old standards maintained.

The Jews who returned to the land faced many diffi-
culties and hardships. Quarrels erupted between the Jews
who stayed in Babylon and the returned exiles because
they laid claim to the same lands. There were also strong
differences among the returned exiles themselves. The
question of priorities arose as well. Should they build
the walls of the city first, or should they build the temple
immediately?

There were other problems. The surrounding nations
were determined to thwart Cyrus's decree. During the
captivity they had encroached upon Judean territory and
encouraged intermarriage between the Jews and their
own people. They realized that if the temple were built
and Jerusalem surrounded by walls, their influence in
the Persian court would end, so they wrote a letter to the
king of Persia charging the Jews with rebellion. The king
immediately ordered Zerubbabel to stop building the
wall.

The Judeans were also opposed by the Samaritans.

They were a people who lived in the north of Judea. While the Jews were in Babylon, the Samaritans infiltrated the territory vacated by the Jews. The Samaritans now demanded the right to participate in the rebuilding of the temple because they were descendants of the northern tribes of Israel, whose kingdom had been destroyed in 722 B.C. But the Samaritans were a mixed people, having intermarried with the Cuthites. The Cuthites worshiped other gods and the Jews had learned their lesson: they would no longer compromise with idolatry.

It looked like a stalemate. The Jews had returned, but they could not rebuild their temple. Neither could they get the land to yield good crops because it had remained untilled for so long. The exiles became discouraged and indifferent and some regretted leaving Babylon. Others forgot their goal of rebuilding the temple and built their own houses instead.

At that point God sent His prophets who proclaimed that the harvests would once more become abundant and the poverty of the Jews would cease if they would put the Lord's service before their own needs and at once begin to rebuild the temple. Haggai thundered:

> This is what the Lord Almighty says: "These people say, 'The time has not yet come for the Lord's house to be built.'"
>
> Then the word of the Lord came through the prophet Haggai: "Is it a time for you yourselves to be living in your paneled houses, while this house remains a ruin?"
>
> Now this is what the Lord Almighty says: "Give careful thought to your ways. You have planted much, but have harvested little. You eat, but never have enough. You drink, but never have your fill. You put on clothes, but are not warm. You earn wages, only to put them in a purse with holes in it" (Haggai 1:2-6).

Haggai's message had an immediate effect: "So the

Lord stirred up the spirit of Zerubbabel" (Haggai 1:14). Once more the Jews began work on the temple and in 516 B.C.— exactly seventy years after the first temple had been destroyed and about twenty-one years after the first exiles had returned—the rebuilt temple was dedicated.

There was great rejoicing at the dedication of the temple. The people crowded the temple mount to watch the priests offer sacrifices and once more the Levitical choir sang the Psalms. But not all rejoiced. The old men wept. In their youth they had seen the first temple in all its glory and compared to it, the new temple seemed just the shadow of a shade. To these old men Haggai wrote a message of comfort that was fulfilled by our Lord:

> This is what the Lord Almighty says: "In a little while I will once more shake the heavens and the earth, the sea and the dry land. I will shake all nations, and the desired of all nations will come, and I will fill this house with glory," says the Lord Almighty. "The silver is mine and the gold is mine," declares the Lord Almighty. "The glory of this present house will be greater than the glory of the former house," says the Lord Almighty. "And in this place I will grant peace," declares the Lord Almighty (Haggai 2:6-9).

At last the temple was rebuilt, but peace was not yet given, nor would it be available until the Prince of Peace—"the desired of all nations"—came, "making peace through his blood, shed on the cross" (Colossians 1:20).

The Decree of Artaxerxes

More Jews returned to Jerusalem when Artaxerxes was king of Persia. But as we study the history of the Jewish people from the exile to the Messiah, we must remember that the great majority of the Jewish people have never returned to Israel. They are still in the *golus,* the "diaspora or exile." Only a remnant returned from Babylon during the reigns of Cyrus and Artaxerxes.

Although there were many priests who returned with Joshua and Zerubbabel to Jerusalem, there were many more who remained in Babylonia. Centuries later Herod the Great (who through marriage had a legally valid claim to the high priesthood) appointed Hananeel from Babylonia to be his puppet high priest.

The best known among the priests who remained in Babylonia was Ezra. Ezra 7:12 describes him as "Ezra the priest, a scribe of the law of the God of heaven" (KJV), but we do not have any Biblical record of Ezra officiating as a priest. It is as a scribe that we gratefully honor Ezra as one of the most influential Jews in history.

In Old Testament times many of the people were literate; many could read and write, but fluency was rare. There was little opportunity to study the Scriptures because so few copies were available. Jeremiah, as a member of a priestly family, probably received the best education available, but he used a scribe named Baruch to write his prophecies in a scroll (Jeremiah 36:4,32).

A scribe not only copied the Scriptures; he had to know what was in them. Ellison wrote:

> A scribe like Ezra was not simply responsible for the copying of the Scriptures; in one way that was the least of his responsibilities. He had to guarantee that the copies were accurate, which in turn virtually demanded his knowing the Scriptures, or at least the more important sections by heart, so that where the eye or ear was deceived the memory would not be. It was no mere feat of learning by heart. Means were devised by which the memory was aided in obtaining an intelligent grasp of the Scriptures. If the modern view is correct that many of the men of Qumran spent much of their time copying the Scriptures and other religious books, not merely for the community but also for sale outside, it shows

what stress was laid on the work being done by suitable men. Such a one was Ezra.[7]

While the Persians never gave their subject peoples a trace of political freedom, they granted complete religious freedom and insisted on the proper enforcement of the various religious systems. In the case of the Jews, Ezra was given the responsibility of enforcing the laws of God. Ellison wrote:

> This is the first example of what we today call the "millet" system that has come down to us. It has existed in Palestine and in the Near-East ever since. It meant that every recognized religious community was given the right to regulate its own affairs and enforce its own internal religious laws, so long as they did not conflict with the laws of the sovereign state. In other words, what was implicit in Cyrus' permission for the return to build the Temple had now become explicit. Palestinian Jewry had become a religious body and was no longer a national state. The change of status was marked by the special privileges given to the religious functionaries ([Ezra] 7:24). From now on the high priest became the representative and real ruler of Judean Jewry, and this led to his becoming increasingly the head of Jewry at large.[8]

It is now generally believed that the Persian ruler Artaxerxes had a sort of department of state and that Ezra was the head of the Jewish section of its ministry of religious affairs. The king issued orders to the scribe, and Ezra 7 quotes Artaxerxes' decree:

> This is a copy of the letter King Artaxerxes had given to Ezra the priest and teacher, a man learned in matters concerning the commands and decrees of the Lord for Israel:...

Now I decree that any of the Israelites in my kingdom, including priests and Levites, who wish to go to Jerusalem with you, may go. You are sent by the king and his seven advisers to inquire about Judah and Jerusalem with regard to the Law of your God, which is in your hand. Moreover, you are to take with you the silver and gold that the king and his advisers have freely given to the God of Israel, whose dwelling is in Jerusalem, together with all the silver and gold you may obtain from the province of Babylon, as well as the freewill offerings of the people and priests.…

And you, Ezra, in accordance with the wisdom of your God, which you possess, appoint magistrates and judges to administer justice to all the people of Trans-Euphrates—all who know the laws of your God. And you are to teach any who do not know them. Whoever does not obey the law of your God and the law of the king must surely be punished by death, banishment, confiscation of property, or imprisonment (7:11,13-16,25-26).

Ezra's assignment was to go to Jerusalem and organize the religious life of the Jews in compliance with the Law of God, a copy of which he took with him (Ezra 7:14). Ezra was accompanied by nearly two thousand Jews from Babylonia, among whom were a large number of priests, Levites, and temple servants. His commission was threefold: he was to investigate the religious conditions of Jerusalem and Judah; he was to take with him the gifts of the Babylonian Jews as well as the Persian subsidies for the temple; and, most important, he was to appoint magistrates and judges and teach the laws of God.

Ezra and his caravan began their long journey, trusting in the Lord for protection. He had refused to ask the king for a military escort. In Ezra 8:21-23 he wrote:

There, by the Ahava Canal, I proclaimed a fast, so that we might humble ourselves before our God and ask him for a safe journey for us and our children, with all our possessions. I was ashamed to ask the king for soldiers and horsemen to protect us from enemies on the road, because we had told the king, "The gracious hand of our God is on everyone who looks to him, but his great anger is against all who forsake him." So we fasted and petitioned our God about this, and he answered our prayer.

When Ezra arrived safely in Jerusalem after an arduous four-months' journey, it was because the good hand of his God was upon him (Ezra 7:9). When a capable colleague was appointed as his assistant, it was because the good hand of his God was upon him (8:18). Five centuries later Paul wrote about the hand of the Lord: "But concerning Israel he says, 'All day long I have held out my hands to a disobedient and obstinate people" (Romans 10:21).

The ministry of Ezra was another indication of our Lord's outstretched hands. If it were not for Ezra's faithfulness, the returned remnant would have disappeared because of intermarriage and its attendant evils. Fifty years after the temple had been rebuilt, the spiritual and social conditions in Jerusalem were deplorable. Bruce wrote:

> The old curse of the land in the days of the great prophets, moneylending and the consequent reduction of insolvent debtors to the status of serfs, had appeared again. The small-holders had not only to maintain themselves by the produce of their land; they had to pay the temple tax and an imperial tax as well, and many of them were driven to mortgage their fields, vineyards and houses to their wealthier neighbors to raise the money. When they were unable to repay the loans, they were forced to sell their children into serfdom.[9]

When Ezra returned to Jerusalem he was shocked by what he saw and heard. He wrote:

The leaders came to me and said, "The people of Israel, including the priests and the Levites, have not kept themselves separate from the neighboring peoples with their detestable practices, like those of the Canaanites, Hittites, Perizzites, Jebusites, Ammonites, Moabites, Egyptians and Amorites. They have taken some of their daughters as wives for themselves and their sons, and have mingled the holy race with the peoples around them. And the leaders and officials have led the way in this unfaithfulness."

When I heard this, I tore my tunic and cloak, pulled hair from my head and beard and sat down appalled (Ezra 9:1-3).

Ezra prayed and the people repented. Spiritual and social conditions improved under Ezra's teaching of the law of God.

Years later in Nehemiah 8 we see him reading the Law of Moses to the people gathered in the square before the water gate in Jerusalem. It was the feast of trumpets, now celebrated as Rosh Hashanah, the Jewish New Year. The water gate, not one of the city gates, evidently led to the former royal palace, which was south of the temple. The square was so near the temple that the people assembled there could watch the morning sacrifices. Since the square was not sacred ground, everybody could attend "the assembly, which was made up of men and women and all who were able to understand" (Nehemiah 8:2). Solomon Grayzel described what they saw and heard:

On the first of Tishri (Rosh Hashanah) of the year 444 B.C.E., a large number of people gathered in the court of the Temple. They watched with deep interest the priests and Levites at the service and the offering of the sacrifices. When the sacrifices had been completed, all eyes turned to the platform which had been erected in the middle of the court. Nehemiah stood there with the elders of the community and the chief priests. On it arose the dignified figure of Ezra, now an old man. In his hand was a scroll. Silence fell over the multitude as the old man raised his voice. Ezra read of God's covenant with Abraham, of the scene at Mount Sinai, of the warning given to the Hebrews that they must be a holy people, and of the religious and social laws by which that holiness was to be attained. Hours passed, and Ezra still read on. The people gave him close attention, for they were listening to their history, their destiny and their hopes. Their eyes filled with quiet tears when they thought of the great achievements expected of them. Long past midday Ezra stopped. He dismissed the people and told them to celebrate the holiday joyfully. The leaders and priests, deeply moved by the reading, stayed behind. One by one they came and made a solemn pledge to Ezra and Nehemiah to adopt the Torah from which Ezra had been reading as the fundamental law, the Constitution, of the restored state.[10]

After Ezra finished reading the book of the Law of Moses, the day was climaxed when the Levites "instructed the people in the Law while the people were standing there. They read from the Book of the Law of God, making it clear and giving the meaning so that the people could understand what was being read" (Nehemiah 8:7-8). In order to understand the significance of these verses we need to realize that up until then copies of the Scriptures were scarce. It seems that in the days of Josiah there was only one copy of the book of Deuteronomy and it was kept in the temple, where it was discovered by Hilkiah (see 2 Kings 22:8; 2 Chronicles 34:14-15).

Until the time of Ezra it was almost impossible for the Jews to study the Scriptures. They only heard the Law of God at the pilgrim feasts (Deuteronomy 31:10-13). Ellison wrote: "There can be no doubt that the week-long festivals of Passover and Tabernacles were partly spent in re-hearing at least the more important sections of the law."[11]

The other way the Jews heard the Scriptures is the way most Christians first hear the gospel: from their fathers. Exodus 12:26-27 instructs the fathers: "And when your children ask you, 'What does this ceremony mean to you?' then tell them, 'It is the Passover sacrifice to the Lord, who passed over the houses of the Israelites in Egypt and spared our homes when he struck down the Egyptians.'" It is generally accepted that this oral instruction formed the most important part of a Jewish boy's education. Teaching and preaching are still God's method of proclaiming both the law and the gospel.

Nehemiah 8:7-8 records the first expository preaching. The Levites orally explained the written Law so that the people would realize that the Law of God was addressed to each of them individually and not merely to their leaders. The Jews were to become "the people of the Book."

Ezra, inspired by God, taught the Israelites the Word of God orally. Thus the oral tradition began. But in traditional Judaism the rabbis teach that when the Levites orally explained the Law to the people, their interpretation was part of the revelation to Moses and that this interpretation was orally transmitted from generation to generation. The *Encyclopedia Judaica* defines the oral law as

> the authoritative interpretation of the Written Law (Torah, which is the text of the Pentateuch) which was regarded as given to Moses on Sinai, and therefore coexistent with the Written Law. This view of the Oral Law was a fundamental principle of the rabbis. The Written and Oral Laws constitute together "two that are one." It is related that a certain man stood before Shammai and said "Rabbi, How many Torahs have you?" The rabbi replied "Two—one written and one oral."...There is a strong and close bond between the Written Law and

the Oral Law, and neither can exist without the other—both from the dogmatic point of view and from that of historical reality. The Oral Law depends upon the Written Law, but at the same time, say the rabbis, it is clear that there can be no real existence for the Written Law without the Oral.[12]

The oral tradition was abused by the rabbis and priests and became their method of adding to the Scriptures by teaching their interpretations in addition to the Torah. Jesus said, "Thus you nullify the word of God for the sake of your tradition" (Matthew 15:6).

Nehemiah 8 marks a turning point in the history of Israel. Until then the Scriptures had been in the possession of the priests. They had the only copies. Ezra the scribe gave the Scriptures to the people. The rabbis claim that it was Ezra who initiated rigid principles of transcribing, which from that time until today the scribes have so minutely observed that we can be sure their copies of God's Word are accurate.

THE DIASPORA

The Jews lived for just over two hundred years under Persia. In fact the Old Testament closes with the Jews under Persian rule. This period was crucial for the people of Israel. Since only a small percentage of the Jews returned to Jerusalem, the great majority were still scattered all over the Persian world, which extended from the Ganges to the Nile rivers.

The Decline of Persia

An indication of the condition of the Jews in Persia is found in the book of Esther, which vividly describes life in the empire during its decline. The story opens with an account of a luxurious feast staged by the king "for all his nobles and officials. The military leaders of Persia and Media, the princes, and the nobles of the provinces were present" (Esther 1:3). The king is Ahasuerus (KJV) or Xerxes (NIV) in Ezra 4:6 and the book of Esther. Arno C. Gaebelein wrote:

> The name Ahasuerus is an appelative, which means the chief king, or the king of all kings. Xerxes, the son of Darius Hystaspes, bore this title, king of kings. This title is also given to him in the cuneiform inscriptions. One of these reads as follows: "I, the mighty king, king of kings, king of populous countries, king of this great and mighty earth, far and near."[13]

The Bible describes Ahasuerus as "the Xerxes who ruled over 127 provinces stretching from India to Cush" (Esther 1:1). Xerxes had three capital cities, but he was proudest of his winter capital, "the citadel of Susa" (1:5). Scripture gives us a glimpse of the opulence of his winter palace:

> The garden had hangings of white and blue linen, fastened with cords of white linen and purple material to silver rings on marble pillars. There were couches of gold and silver on a mosaic pavement of porphyry, marble, mother-of-pearl and other costly stones. Wine was served in goblets of gold (Esther 1:6-7).

Xerxes "ruled over 127 provinces from India to Cush," but one night he couldn't sleep (Esther 6:1). God was to show the enemies of the Jews who the King of kings really is! The book of Esther was written to demonstrate that Xerxes was not king of kings. It was written to the Jewish people who were scattered all over the Persian world and who were facing a seemingly certain extinction.

During this period of decline the prestige of the high priest increased enormously. Bruce wrote:

He was not only at the head of the temple ritual; he became in practice head of the Jewish state in all that concerned its internal affairs, the more so as the Jewish state was now a temple-state, and this position was retained by the high priest, apart from a few exceptional intervals, throughout the era of the Second Temple.[14]

The Development of the Synagogue

At this stage in history we notice a duality in the Jews' religious existence. It was centered in the temple in Jerusalem, but worship apart from the temple was also recognized.

This duality developed because the great majority of the Jews were still in exile. Only those Jews in Persia who were wealthy enough to make pilgrimages to Jerusalem could participate in the temple festivals, so the question was, How are the rest of the Jews in the dispersion to continue to worship the God of Abraham, Isaac, and Jacob? The answer to this question was the synagogue. *The Encyclopedia of the Jewish Religion* states:

> The exact origin of the synagogue is unknown. Though prayer was an integral part of sacrificial service at an early time...there is no record of the existence of special prayer houses. The synagogue may have originated during the period of Babylonian captivity, although some scholars trace its beginnings to the period of the Kingdom. The first Babylonian exiles (597 B.C.E.) seem to have met for the purpose of exposition of the Scriptures and public worship on Sabbaths and festivals; when the bulk of the people were exiled to Babylonia (586 B.C.E.) they already found the institution of meeting for prayer and instruction in existence. Such gatherings are recorded in the Book of Ezekiel, and the reference in Ezek. 11:16 possibly reflects the

emergence of the synagogue in the Babylonian Exile. To the allegation of the inhabitants of Jerusalem that the exiles, being far removed from the Temple, had forfeited the presence and protection of God, the prophet replied with the Divine message that God Himself would be a *mikdash me'at* ("a little sanctuary") to Israel in exile (Ezek. 11:15-16). This was interpreted by the rabbis to refer to the "houses of worship and houses of learning."[15]

One of the most important results of the Jewish exile in Persia was the development of the synagogue. The origin of the synagogue is obscure. However, we believe that the rabbis are correct when they say that it was Ezra who instituted what has now become the liturgy of the synagogue. There are some elements of synagogue worship that have persisted from Ezra's time until now. A study of Nehemiah 8 will clearly validate this fact.

When Ezra read the Law to the Israelites who had returned, "all the people [were] assembled...in the square before the Water Gate" (Nehemiah 8:1)—not in the temple. It was at this assembly that worship outside of the temple was recognized. Now Jews all over the Persian empire could worship apart from the temple.

The most important element in the synagogue service is the reading from the Law. Ezra was called by the people to read the Law, and it has always been the custom in the synagogue for the congregation to call upon someone to read a portion of the Law. Readings from the Prophets were subsequently added to the liturgy. Eventually our Lord "went to Nazareth, where he had been brought up, and on the Sabbath day he went into the synagogue, as was his custom. And he stood up to read. The scroll of the prophet Isaiah was handed to him" (Luke 4:16-17).

When Ezra read the Law, he "stood on a high wooden platform built for the occasion" (Nehemiah 8:4) and from earliest times it has been customary for the reader to stand on the platform *(bema)* in the center of the synagogue.

When Ezra opened the Torah, "the people all stood

up" (8:5), and this standing up of the people is still the custom in the synagogue.

"Ezra praised the Lord, the great God; and all the people lifted their hands and responded, 'Amen! Amen!'" (8:6). The *Mishnah* says, "He who begins the Torah reading, and he who finishes it, utters a blessing before and after" (Mishnah: Megilla 4:1; Talmud: Megilla 21a). The "Amen" response is still followed in orthodox synagogues.

In a short review of redemption history we can recognize the hand of God in the development of the synagogue. It has always been the purpose of God that all men everywhere would worship Him. When mankind failed at the tower of Babel, God chose the Jewish nation to fulfill His purpose. The Lord said to Abraham, "I will bless those who bless you, and whoever curses you I will curse; and all peoples on earth will be blessed through you" (Genesis 12:3). The student of the New Testament Scriptures gladly recognizes that our Lord's great commission to "make disciples of all nations" (Matthew 28:19) is inherent in the Abrahamic covenant.

In spite of God's gracious calling, the descendants of Abraham sinned against God. Time after time our Lord remonstrated with them: "From the time your forefathers left Egypt until now, day after day, again and again I sent you my servants and prophets. But they did not listen to me or pay attention. They were stiff-necked and did more evil than their forefathers" (Jeremiah 7:25-26).

Finally judgment came. Jerusalem and the temple were destroyed and the Jewish people were scattered all over the Babylonian empire. It was a terrible day, but even in judgment God showed His mercy. In Babylon the Jews learned their lesson. Scribes made copies of the Scriptures and the Jews began to meet on the Sabbath to study the book of the Law and the Prophets.

Persia defeated Babylon and some of the Jews returned and rebuilt the temple. But the vast majority of the Jews were (and still are) dispersed all over the world. Wherever in the world there were ten or more Jewish men, there was a synagogue. These synagogues became lighthouses in the stormy sea of paganism.

Daniel 2:21 says that God "sets up kings and deposes them." In the same chapter of Daniel we read the prophecy of the great statue. The head of gold represented Babylon. The chest and arms of silver represented Persia. Under Persia, Jewish history was divided into two streams: the Jews in Jerusalem and Judea, and the Jews dispersed all over the world. In the providence of God these two streams enriched and nourished each other.

Four centuries later "when the time had fully come, God sent his Son" (Galatians 4:4). His commission was to make disciples of all nations. When the disciples went to all nations, they went "to the Jew first, and also to the Greek" (Romans 1:16, KJV). They went to the synagogues that were scattered all over the world and in them found many Gentiles who had become "devout converts to Judaism" (Acts 13:43; also see Acts 14:1; 17:4,12). When the apostles turned to the Gentiles, they did not have to leave the synagogue.

How did this happen? The answer is that God was not inactive in intertestamental history. He set up Nebuchadnezzar and deposed him. He set up Cyrus and used him. He set up Xerxes and under him "many people of other nationalities became Jews" (Esther 8:17). Persia lasted just two hundred years, for God was going to set up and depose another king. Remember that Daniel had mentioned another empire: Greece, the belly and thighs of bronze of the statue in Nebuchadnezzar's dream.

Our story so far has taken place in Asia and Africa. Away to the north and west, on the coast of the Mediterranean sea, many small city-states had been battling each other for over a century. Eventually a leader would arise who would include these city-states in one empire and change world history. Daniel 8:5 calls him "a goat with a prominent horn between his eyes." God was going to set up and depose Alexander the Great. Again Palestine would become the battleground of the world's armies.

4

The Jewish Nation under Greece

THE FALL OF PERSIA

Old Testament history is the story of two civilizations, each of which thrived around the deltas
of great rivers. In the East the Mesopotamian civilization grew around the delta of the Tigris and Euphrates
rivers, which flow into what is now known as the Persian
Gulf. Fifteen hundred miles to the west another great
civilization rose around the delta of the Nile river, which
empties into the Mediterranean sea. The only feasible
corridor through which these two cultures could com-
municate—for trade or war—was the "fertile crescent,"
which is the fertile green area that extends northwest
from the Persian Gulf along the Tigris and Euphrates
rivers and then dips southward into Canaan.

Abraham was born in Ur of the Chaldees, near the
confluence of the Tigris and Euphrates rivers. When he
was seventy-five years old, he followed the fertile crescent to Haran and from there he migrated to Canaan
(see Genesis 11:31). From Canaan Abraham migrated
to Egypt and later he returned from Egypt to Canaan.
The road traveled by Abraham was the same route taken

by the nations in the Old Testament world. When the Assyrians or the Babylonians attacked Egypt, and when Egypt attacked the Assyrians, the only feasible route for their armies passed through Canaan, which is now the nation of Israel.

With the ascendancy of Persia, a different area of potential conquest beckoned. When Cyrus the Great began his campaign for world dominion, he defeated Croesus in Lydia. This kingdom was in western Asia Minor (now western Turkey). In Lydia there were a number of Greek settlements. The Greeks in Lydia maintained very close ties with their kinsmen in Europe just across the Aegean sea.

The Greeks in Europe lived in independent city-states. Cyrus realized that if Persia was to rule the world, he would eventually have to conquer these city-states as well as Lydia. Sooner or later Persia would have to fight the European Greeks.

Both Cyrus and Darius the Great made abortive attempts to crush the city-states of Greece. All these kings did was to unite the city-states for a time (usually there was fierce rivalry among them). When the Ionians revolted, Darius determined to bring the city-states of mainland Greece into his empire. He sent an expedition to Athens, but it ended in failure at the battle of Marathon in 490 B.C.

Xerxes, who was thirty-five years old when he succeeded Darius, faced two problems at the beginning of his reign: the Greek cities were continually revolting, and the land of Egypt thought that this was a good time for a revolt. Xerxes decided to handle his problems one at a time. First he subdued Egypt. Then Babylon also revolted and Xerxes cruelly demolished their temple. (From then on, the Persian kings used "king of Babylon" as part of their royal title. Xerxes called himself "king of Persia and Media.") Now Xerxes felt it was time to attack Greece. He carefully planned his approach by both land and sea. Will Durant wrote:

Xerxes prepared leisurely but thoroughly for the second Persian attack upon Greece. For four years he collected troops and materials from all the provinces of his realm; and when, in 481, he at last set forth, his army was probably the largest ever assembled in history before our own century. Herodotus reckoned it, without moderation, at 2,641,000 fighting men, and an equal number of engineers, slaves, merchants, provisioners, and prostitutes; he tells us, with perhaps a twinkle in his eye, that when Xerxes' army drank water whole rivers ran dry. It was, naturally and fatally, a highly heterogeneous force. There were Persians, Medes, Babylonians, Afghans, Indians, Bactrians, Sogdians, Sacae, Assyrians, Armenians, Colchians, Scyths, Paeonians, Mysians, Paphlagonians, Phrygians, Thracians, Thessalians, Locrians, Boeotians, Aeolians, Ionians, Lydians, Carians, Cilicians, Cypriotes, Phoenicians, Syrians, Arabians, Egyptians, Ethiopians, Libyans, and many more. There were footmen, cavalrymen, chariots, elephants, and a fleet of transports and fighting triremes numbering, according to Herodotus, 1207 ships in all. When Greek spies were caught in the camp, and a general ordered their execution, Xerxes countermanded the order, spared the men, had them conducted through his forces, and then set them free, trusting that when they had reported to Athens and Sparta the extent of his preparations, the remainder of Greece would hasten to surrender.[1]

In the spring of 480 B.C. the Persian hordes reached Hellespont (now called the Dardanelles), the narrow strait that separates Asia Minor from Europe. The Egyptian and Phoenician engineers in Xerxes' army built a bridge of ships across the strait. According to Herodotus the bridge was constructed of 674 ships, each moored with a heavy anchor. Xerxes' men made cables of flax and papyrus, bound the cables to the ships, and made the cables taut by using capstans. Trees were cut and planks were laid across the cables. The planks were covered with earth, and the bridge became a road that was one of the outstanding engineering feats of all time. In one week the entire Persian host crossed the Hellespont from Asia into Europe.

Imagine the terror of the Greeks as this horde advanced. Sparta, Athens, and the other Greek city-states united, but at first it seemed that defense was futile. Athens was occupied and the Greek refugees fled with the Greek navy to Salamis. There the Greeks trapped the Persians and destroyed an entire corps as well as the Persian navy! Xerxes' army retreated and was defeated at Plataea in 479 B.C.

If the Greeks had not defeated Persia, the development of Europe would have been very different. The fall of Xerxes ushered in a new era of redemption history.

Xerxes was a great king, as kings go, but his father Darius spoke of a greater King: "He is the living God and he endures forever; his kingdom will not be destroyed, his dominion will never end" (Daniel 6:26).

All students of history realize the importance of the Greek-Persian wars. A believer in the Scriptures realizes much more: Persia was the second world empire prophesied by Daniel and the third was Greece (Daniel 2:32).

Two centuries before Alexander the Great defeated Persia, Daniel had a vision: "In my vision I saw myself in the citadel of Susa [this is where Esther became the queen]....There before me was a ram with two horns....A goat with a prominent horn between his eyes came from the west, crossing the whole earth without touching the ground" (Daniel 8:2-5). Gabriel interpreted Daniel's vision: "The two-horned ram that you saw represents the kings of Media and Persia. The shaggy goat is the king of Greece, and the large horn between his eyes is the first king" (8:20-21). The meteoric rise of the first king is foretold in Daniel 11:2-3:

Three more kings will appear in Persia, and then a fourth, who will be far richer than all the others. When he has gained power by his wealth, he will stir up everyone against the kingdom of Greece. Then a mighty king will appear, who will rule with great power and do as he pleases.

THE RISE OF GREECE

Historians do not know much about the origin of the Greeks. Like the Persians, they were Aryan. Evidently they originally lived in Asia Minor and Crete. About the same time that Moses led the Israelites out of Egypt, the Greeks invaded the Aegean peninsula.

Greek history properly begins in the seventh century B.C. when the city-states of Athens, Sparta, and Corinth were founded. The land separating these city-states from each other was mountainous. There were many rivers, bridges were rare, and the roads were poor. Besides these geographical barriers there were tribal differences. The Athenians despised the Spartans and both hated the Corinthians.

In the fifth and fourth centuries B.C. these city-states produced many great leaders in almost every field of learning. These centuries were Greece's golden age.

Greece's golden age was also its age of terror. Xerxes was extending the Persian empire to Asia Minor and the Mediterranean world, and Greece was next on his timetable. Max I. Dimont wrote:

> There was no question as to who would annihilate whom. There was no logical reason for a supposition that the tiny Greek city-states would defeat the colossus from the East, but that is precisely what happened at the famed land battle at Marathon (490 B.C.) and the equally famed sea battle at Salamis (480 B.C.) where the Greeks shattered the vastly superior Persian forces. It was illogical, but as history never

stops to apologize for her inconsistencies, she continued to be illogical and permitted the Greek tribes to defeat the Persian armies over and over again.

In between beating the Persians, the Greeks went back to their favorite pastime—fighting among themselves. It never occurred to them to pursue the defeated enemy into his homeland. The Greeks thought their civilization too good for the barbarians. Why invade and be burdened with the problem of governing and educating them?

Alexander the Great was the first Greek on record who had different ideas on that point. He dreamed of a world empire. In 334 B.C. he crossed the Hellespont with 32,000 infantrymen and shattered the armies of an empire which had millions of soldiers at its command. The Persian armies were first defeated at the River Granicus, then annihilated at the Battle of Issus, where Alexander demanded the unconditional surrender of Darius III. The Persian Empire ceased to exist. By the law of "winner takes all," the Jews passed under Greek rule.[2]

Strictly speaking, Alexander was not a Greek. He was a Macedonian. Culturally, however, he was passionately Greek. He was educated by Aristotle himself. Durant wrote:

Perhaps it was the philosopher who instilled into the mind of the youth that ardor for unity which gave some grandeur to Alexander's victories; more probably that resolve descended to him from his father's ambitions, and was fused into a passion by his maternal blood. If we would understand Alexander we must always remember that he bore in his veins the drunken vigor of Philip and the barbaric intensity of Olympias. Furthermore, Olympias claimed descent from Achilles. Therefore the *Iliad* had a special fascination for Alexander; when he crossed the Hellespont he was, in his interpretation, retracing the steps of Achilles; when he conquered Hither Asia he was completing the work that his ancestor had begun at Troy. Through all his campaigns he carried with him a copy of the *Iliad* annotated by Aristotle; often he placed it under his pillow at night beside his dagger, as if to symbolize the instrument and the goal.[3]

To the Jews in Jerusalem and to the Jews scattered throughout the world, Alexander's conquests portended a bitter struggle. It would be Aristotle against Moses, the *Iliad* versus the Prophets.

Alexander was a passionate missionary: he was the apostle of Hellenism. His ambition was not only to establish a Greek empire, but also to control this vast empire by extending Hellenic culture to all men everywhere. He wanted everybody to speak Greek, think Greek, and act Greek.

The Greeks were convinced that they were the only civilized people. Alexander believed that by spreading Hellenic culture he was liberating the world. One of the strategies he used to extend Greek civilization was to build cities as centers from which his gospel would penetrate the environs. H. L. Ellison wrote:

> The centre of cultured Greek life had always been the city, the *polis*. The Hellenistic rulers never tried to impose a mass Greek civilization on their subjects; they could not have, even had they wanted to. They relied on their cities gradually to extend their civilizing influence over the countryside around. As the life of the *polis* had developed, it was essentially one for the cultured gentleman who had slaves to enable him to have sufficient leisure to give himself to polite pursuits. So we have to picture Hellenism as spreading from the city to the village, from the rich to the poor. The fact that most of the Jews in Judea were probably farmers with few slaves to give them leisure helps to explain why the

majority were slow to be influenced by the new outlook on life.[4]

Another method that Alexander used to propagate Hellenism was intermarriage. He married the daughter of Darius at a great nuptial feast in Susa in 324 B.C. Eighty of his officers took Persian brides at the same time. Thousands of similar marriages were arranged for his soldiers. He gave each officer a substantial dowry and paid the debts of the marrying soldiers.

Alexander's culminating ruse was religious. In 324 B.C. he proclaimed his deity, saying he was the son of Zeus-Ammon. But his mortality was soon evident. Durant described his untimely death:

> Back in Babylon, he abandoned himself more and more to drink. One night, reveling with his officers, he proposed a drinking match. Promachus quaffed twelve quarts of wine, and won the prize, a talent; three days later he died. Shortly afterward, at another banquet, Alexander drained a goblet containing six quarts of wine. On the next night he drank heavily again; and cold weather suddenly setting in, he caught a fever, and took to his bed. The fever raged for ten days during which Alexander continued to give orders to his army and his fleet. On the eleventh day he died, being in the thirty-third year of his age (323). When his generals asked him to whom he left his empire he answered, "To the strongest."[5]

Alexander died in 323 B.C., but his religion still flourishes today. For two centuries after Alexander's death, Jewish history became a struggle between Hellenism with its attractive pleasures of both mind and body, and the ethical monotheism of the Scriptures.

The life and death of Alexander the Great were foretold in Daniel 11—one of the most remarkable prophecies in the Bible. Verses 3-35 give a synopsis of Jewish history from Alexander, who wrested the Holy Land from

Persia in 330 B.C., to the great persecution of the Jews by Antiochus Epiphanes, who desecrated the temple in 168 B.C. When we remember that Daniel recorded this prophecy in 534 B.C.—almost four centuries before some of the prophesied events took place—we realize that prophecy is actually prewritten history. Note how accurately each detail of Daniel 11:3-4 was fulfilled.

"A mighty king will appear." This king was Alexander the Great.

He "will rule with great power." A legend states that Alexander wept because he had no more worlds to conquer.

He will "do as he pleases." Twice Darius offered to negotiate a very favorable treaty, but Alexander did not want negotiations; he demanded victory.

"After he has appeared, his empire will be broken up and parceled out toward the four winds of heaven. It will not go to his descendants." After the death of Alexander the Great there was a fierce struggle for his empire. There were two legal heirs: a half-witted half brother, Philip; and a son by Roxana, unborn at Alexander's death and later named Alexander. Neither heir had a chance. F. F. Bruce described what happened:

> Within a few years Philip Arrhidaeus and his wife Eurydice had been put to death by Olympias; Olympias in turn was put to death by Cassander, son of Antipater, who controlled Macedonia and Greece, and later on Cassander also murdered Roxana and her young son, Alexander. As all Alexander's legitimate heirs had thus been removed, there was no longer any need to maintain the pretense of guardianship and regency, and a scramble began for the succession.[6]

Alexander's empire finally was divided by his four generals. Ptolemy ruled Egypt in the south; Seleucus's empire extended north and east beyond Babylon; Lysimachus ruled farther north in what is now Turkey;

and Cassander ruled Greece in the west. (In describing this division we have used Israel as the hub because it was the major source of contention between Seleucus and Ptolemy. Ptolemy claimed Israel as a part of his empire, but Seleucus also wanted it. The tiny nation of Israel, fighting for its own independence, was the land bridge connecting Asia, Europe, and Africa. Israel's strategic importance as a major trade and military route made it a continual battlefield between contending world empires.)

THE JEWS UNDER ALEXANDER

With the victory of Alexander the Great at the battle of Arabela in 330 B.C., the dominion of Palestine passed from Persian into Greek hands. But the Jews had been treated kindly by their Persian rulers, and out of gratitude as well as because of their normal conservatism, they remained faithful to Darius. This loyalty angered Alexander and he determined to destroy Jerusalem as he had already destroyed Gaza. For some unknown reason the Jews did not fight Alexander. Instead Josephus tells us that the high priest led a procession of the people in white garments. This evidently placated Alexander and he became a friend of the Jews. He respected their religion and continued their self-government, which they had enjoyed under the Persians.

The Jews of the dispersion, who were given liberty and freedom of commerce, settled in many places throughout the empire. Their faithfulness in the worship of Jehovah was the first witness that the heathen world received of the one true God. And the descendants of these Jews were the first to be contacted when Christian missionaries went "to the Jew first" as they traveled from city to city founded by Alexander. Little did he realize that he was merely a pawn in the hands of the great One of Israel.

And when Alexander made Greek the universal language, he was preparing the way of our Lord! The Old

Testament Scriptures were translated from Hebrew into Greek and became the property of the world. Later the Gospels could be understood in the uttermost parts of the earth without preliminary language study.

THE JEWS UNDER THE PTOLEMIES

Of the four rulers who divided Alexander's kingdom, the two who are important in the history of Israel are Ptolemy in Egypt and Seleucus in Asia. Both of these rulers founded dynasties. Ptolemy's dynasty lasted until 31 B.C.

At first Ptolemy and Seleucus were allies, but it was not long before an implacable cold war existed between them. Frequently open hostilities erupted. The bone of contention was Israel, since it was located between the two warring nations. For 125 years the northern empire (Seleucids) and the southern empire (Ptolemies) fought over the control of Israel. The Judeans, caught in the middle, were forced to pay tribute to whoever was the victor.

Daniel 11 vividly, accurately, and prophetically describes the struggles between these two dynasties and the effect on Israel. In this chapter of Scripture "the king of the North" always refers to a king of the Seleucid dynasty, and "the king of the South" refers to Ptolemy or a member of his dynasty. (If you need a mnemonic device, remember **P**tolemy ruled Egy**pt** in the South and **S**eleucus ruled **S**yria in the North.)

Finally being successful in battle and negotiating a settlement with Seleucus, Ptolemy was able to command Syria and the coastland of Asia as far north as Phoenicia (modern Lebanon). He controlled the great seaports of the eastern Mediterranean as well as Cyprus. He also controlled the land bridge connecting Egypt, Asia, and Europe—the trade routes. In addition Ptolemy ruled Lebanon, which would provide timber for the huge building projects he planned for his capital in Egypt: Alexandria, which was built by Alexander.

Ptolemy was determined to make Alexandria the greatest city in history. The lighthouse he built on the island of Pharos at the entrance to Alexandria's harbor was one of the seven wonders of the ancient world. However, as we shall see, an even brighter light would shine from Pharos!

The Translation of the Hebrew Scriptures

To fulfill his plans (and the plans of the King of kings), Ptolemy, now in control of Jerusalem, feigned faith in the Lord. He then deported a large number of Jews from Jerusalem to Alexandria, where they built a synagogue. The time came when these Jews spoke Greek instead of Hebrew, so in order to understand their worship service, they needed a translation of the Scriptures into Greek. Bruce explained:

> From our point of view, the most important feature of Ptolemy's control of Syria and Phoenicia is the fact that he was thus master of Judaea. Josephus tells how he entered Jerusalem on a sabbath day in 320 B.C., pretending that he wished to offer sacrifice in the temple, and made himself master of the city by force. At that time, too, he deported a considerable number of people from Jerusalem and Judaea, and settled them in Alexandria. There they lived as free men under their own laws, and the attractions of the new city were such that many other Jews soon made their way there voluntarily, until one of the five wards of the city was completely Jewish and they spread into one of the other wards as well. The Jewish community of Alexandria speedily became one of the most important communities of the Diaspora. They formed the most important section of the city's non-Greek population; they were accorded special privileges and had their own constitution as a sort of municipality within a municipality. In Alexandria after one or

two generations the Jews gave up the use of their old Semitic tongue and spoke Greek like their neighbors.[7]

Ptolemy was succeeded by his son Ptolemy II (Philadelphius), who played a role in the translation of the Scriptures. There is a legend preserved in the Letter to Aristeas[8] that tells how Ptolemy II wanted to complete his great library in Alexandria. He ordered Eleazar the high priest to send seventy-two scholars from Jerusalem to Alexandria in order to translate the Torah (the five books of Moses known as the Law) into Greek for the royal library. The translators were given quarters on the island of Pharos. Each translator worked in his own cubicle. The legend states that they all worked on corresponding passages and completed their translations in seventy-two days. When they compared their translations, thirteen of them included identical changes!

One fact is not legendary: during the reign of the Ptolemies the Hebrew Scriptures *were* translated into Greek. Before that time, if a non-Jew wanted to study the Scriptures, he had to learn Hebrew. Probably the synagogues were the only places where the Hebrew Scriptures were available. Once the translation was completed, Gentiles could read the Scriptures in Greek, the universal language of the day. God's Word was available for all: Jew *and* Gentile.

Here we see the Biblical philosophy of history. It had always been God's purpose that all men everywhere would worship Him and now God's Word was available to all men. It was "first for the Jew, then for the Gentile" (Romans 1:16). God was fulfilling His promise to Abraham: "All peoples on earth will be blessed through you" (Genesis 12:3).

The War between the Hellenists and the Prophets

At first life under the Ptolemies was good for Palestinian Jews. As long as they paid their taxes and did not participate in insurrection, they were left alone. They had complete religious freedom. Their government was administered by the high priest, whose power was limited by the Sanhedrin, which acted as both a legislative body and a supreme court.

The Jews outside of Palestine were scattered all over the world. Wherever the Jews went, they built synagogues and remained loyal to the temple in Jerusalem. Every male over twenty years of age paid his temple taxes and made pilgrimages to Jerusalem whenever possible (see Acts 2).

But the Jews of the dispersion were always attracted to the cities, which were the core of Greek culture. In these urban settings the Hebrews were subjected to the influence of Hellenism. Soon there were noticeable differences between the Jews of the diaspora and the Palestinian Jews.

In the cities a war was being waged between the Hellenist philosophers and the prophets of God. For a while it seemed as though the prophets had lost. Although Alexander's successors fought one another bitterly, they were all thoroughly convinced that the Hellenism he espoused was the only way of life. Thus "war" was declared on the Jewish lifestyle.

The Jews in the Greek cities began assuming Greek names, perhaps for business purposes. To be less conspicuous, they abandoned their customary Jewish attire for the more fashionable Greek clothing. Very innocuously the Hellenic language, customs, and culture were introduced and before long Greek morals, ethics, and in many cases religion were gradually accepted. In Palestine most Jews were farmers; in the dispersion many became merchants.

An ancient historian, Posidonius, described life in the Greek cities:

> The people of these cities are relieved by the fertility of their soil from a laborious struggle for existence. Life is a continuous series of social festivities. Their gymnasiums they use as baths where they anoint

themselves with costly oils and myrrhs. In the *qrammateia* (such is the name they give to the public eating-halls) they practically live, filling themselves there for the better part of the day with rich foods and wine; much that they cannot eat they carry away home. They feast to the prevailing music of strings. The cities are filled from end to end with the noise of harp-playing.[9]

But gluttony was not universal. A new physical fitness clique arose and Greek games became popular. Each city erected fine public buildings and the gymnasium was one of the most important. The word *gymnasium* is derived from the Greek *gymnos*, which means "naked." Nude wrestling became commonplace among Jewish young men. Their nakedness revealed the fact of their circumcision, a sign of their covenant with God, so an operation was devised to disguise their circumcision.

Another building in each city was the theater. Dimont wrote of its influence on the Jews:

> The younger set came in contact with the urbane sophistication of the Greeks, and from here the door led to the cabaret and to the couch of the concubine. Soon pleasure was pursued as a policy, and "folly soared into philosophy." The road to apostasy ran from the front pew in the synagogue to a seat in the theater to the embrace of the hetaera to a front pew in a pagan temple.
>
> Just as Jewish businessmen yielded to Greek manners and Jewish youth to Greek pleasure, so the Jewish intellectuals succumbed to the spell of the Greek philosophers, whom the Orthodox Jews regarded with more alarm than they did the courtesans. The latter could corrupt only the body, whereas the former corrupted the mind.
>
> Of all the Greek philosophers, the Epicureans were singled out as special targets for condemnation by the Orthodox Jews. The Epicureans were cynics

who taught that the gods did not intervene in human affairs. They taught that it was man's duty to free himself from such superstitions as punishment and reward, and that there was no such thing as morality and immorality, only pleasure. The pursuit of pleasure, the Epicureans held, was man's only true goal.

Under the impact of the distortions taught by Epicurus, immorality and licentiousness replaced the traditional values of chastity and faithfulness. So threatening were the inroads made by the Epicureans on Jewish youth, that their very name—*Apikoros* in Yiddish—became a dreaded curse so deeply embedded that it persists until this day among Jews.[10]

The great allurement faced by the Jewish people in the Old Testament had been the enticement to the idolatry of the Canaanites. During the intertestamental period, the Hellenistic way of life was Judah's great temptation. And just as there had been a remnant who would not bow their knees to Baal, so there was also a remnant of Judeans who were not enticed by the pleasures of Greece.

THE JEWS UNDER THE SELEUCIDS

The Ptolemies were generally benevolent despots, but the prophecy of Daniel 11:15-16 was fulfilled:

> The king of the North will come and build up siege ramps and will capture a fortified city. The forces of the South will be powerless to resist; even their best troops will not have the strength to stand. The invader will do as he pleases; no one will be able to stand against him. He will establish himself in the Beautiful Land and will have the power to destroy it.

In 275 B.C. the cold war between Ptolemy in the South and Seleucus in the North finally erupted into violent warfare. Ptolemy II invaded northern Syria and was defeated. This war was the first of a series that did not end until 198 B.C. when Antiochus III (called Antiochus the Great) decisively defeated Ptolemy IV's troops at Gaza. As a result of this victory the "king of the North" gained control of all of Syria and Judea as far as Egypt's borders.

Antiochus the Great

Generally Antiochus the Great was a magnanimous king. He permitted the Jews a high degree of self-government under the high priest and the Sanhedrin, and wisely granted the Jews the temple constitution, which the Greeks had continued after conquering Persia in 333 B.C.

But Antiochus the Great had a consuming obsession: he wanted to reunite and rule the empire that Alexander had governed. To try to reach that goal, however, was a futile task. Four centuries before Antiochus the Great, Daniel had prophesied of another kingdom arising. Interpreting Nebuchadnezzar's dream of a large statue with legs of iron, he had said: "Finally, there will be a fourth kingdom, strong as iron—for iron breaks and smashes everything—and as iron breaks things to pieces, so it will crush and break all the others" (Daniel 2:40). And Rome, the legs of iron, began to thwart the plans of Antiochus the Great.

When the Romans finally defeated Hannibal at Zania in 202 B.C., Hannibal fled eastward with his famous elephants and took refuge in the court of Antiochus. Wanting to stir up trouble for Rome, Hannibal encouraged Antiochus to invade Greece. This strategy was disastrous. Rome declared war on Antiochus, expelled him from Greece, and drove him to an ignominious retreat into Asia Minor. There, at the battle of Magnesia, the Romans under Cornelius Supio inflicted a humiliating defeat on Antiochus. He lost his navy and his elephants, and the Romans extorted an enormous retribution from him. Worst of all, in order to make sure that the indemnity would be paid, the younger son of Antiochus the Great was taken to Rome as a hostage.

Antiochus's son stayed in Rome as a hostage for fourteen years. There he learned firsthand about Rome's iron-fisted use of power. In a few decades the Jews would feel his fury. He was called Antiochus IV (Epiphanes).

The death of Antiochus the Great was followed by conflicts among members of the Seleucid family. His son Seleucus IV (Philopator) (Daniel 11:14) was assassinated by his minister Heliodorus (Daniel 11:20). Antiochus Epiphanes, who was released after Demetrius took his place, became the king. Harold A. Sevener in his commentary on Daniel wrote:

> The Hellenist Jews in Jerusalem continued to pressure Seleucus to take the treasure [the temple treasure] rather than to tax the people. However, before Seleucus was able to seize the treasure, Heliodorus, his trusted treasurer, poisoned him (175 B.C.) and attempted to take the throne for himself. Perhaps Seleucus sensed that his life was in danger and that he was in need of help, for he had dispatched his own son, Demetrius, to Rome in exchange for Antiochus Epiphanes IV (Seleucus' brother) who had been taken as a hostage to Rome some fourteen years earlier. In fact, Antiochus Epiphanes was returning to Syria when he heard that his brother, Seleucus, had been murdered by Heliodorus, who had subsequently usurped the throne.
>
> The news of his brother's death infuriated Antiochus....Immediately, Antiochus made political alliances with two men who had been his father's enemies—Eumenes, King of Pergamum, and his brother, Attalas. These two men had supplied

Antiochus with armies and financial aid in his fight against Heliodorus. Before long, the armies of Antiochus prevailed, and Heliodorus was captured and cruelly slain. Demetrius, Seleucus' son and rightful heir to the throne, was left in Rome, and Antiochus proclaimed himself to be the rightful king of Syria and Asia (including Judea).[11]

Antiochus Epiphanes

Antiochus Epiphanes inherited the huge indemnities that were imposed by Rome against his father. One of the first things Antiochus Epiphanes did to raise the money was to sell the high priesthood to the highest bidder. Pfeiffer wrote:

> To Antiochus, the high priesthood was a political office. As Syrian king, he would have the right to appoint whomever he chose. To the pious Jews, however, the priesthood was of divine origin, and its sale to the highest bidder was looked upon as a sin against God. Since the priesthood involved both civil and religious functions, both viewpoints would appear valid to their respective adherents.[12]

In the early days of Antiochus Epiphanes' reign Jerusalem was ruled by the high priest Onias III, a strictly orthodox Jew. The Hellenistic Jews opposed Onias and supported his brother Jason, who had promised Antiochus a huge tribute. Knowing how Antiochus felt, a delegation of Hellenistic Jews visited the Syrian king in 175 B.C. and presented him with a revolutionary proposal, which he eagerly accepted: Onias was to be deposed and imprisoned, Jason was to be declared high priest, and the traditional government by priests and Sanhedrin was to be abolished. Jerusalem would become a Greek-style city-state. The Hellenistic Jews even planned to name Jerusalem "Antioch" after Antiochus Epiphanes! In order to train their sons for government service, they built a gymnasium in sight of the temple and even young priests forsook their temple tasks to exercise in the gymnasium.

For 137 years the Ptolemies and the Seleucids had passionately pursued their Hellenistic campaign. They had been successful all over their empire except in Judea. There they met the stubborn resistance of the Hasideans, a party that had originally been formed as a protest against the pleasure-seeking Epicureans. The Hasideans were not anti-Greek. Their motive was not political; it was moral. They proclaimed the power of the Mosaic law.

But where his predecessors had failed, Antiochus Epiphanes succeeded. And it took a renegade Hellenistic Jew, the false high priest Jason, to ensure his success. The gates of the temple were opened to idolatry. Jewish priests garbed in Greek robes officiated at Greek idolatrous rites.

Antiochus was aided in his effort to make Jerusalem a Greek city by members of leading Jewish families who were eager to enjoy the social, political, and cultural privileges of cities like Alexandria and Antioch. There was no longer any difference between Jew and Greek. The distinction between the ethical monotheism of the Jews and the immoral paganism of the Greeks was eroded. Bruce wrote:

> All this was abhorrent to the old-fashioned pious people of Jerusalem, but there was little they could do to check the tendency which they deplored. These pious people came to be recognized as a definite party—the hasidim (or Hasidaeans, as they are called in the books of Maccabees)—and although they were despised as hopelessly behind the times by the "progressive" elements in the population, the day came when they proved to be the salt of the land and the salvation of their people.[13]

Aided by his appointed high priest, Antiochus plundered the temple treasuries to finance his first war against

Egypt. This act infuriated the conservative Hasideans, but they were only a small minority and they seemed helpless.

Antiochus Epiphanes fought two wars against Egypt. The first was a defensive war and Rome did not interfere. The second was a different story. Daniel had prophesied, "At the appointed time he will invade the South again, but this time the outcome will be different from what it was before" (Daniel 11:29).

Antiochus Epiphanes' victory in the first war went to his head. He decided that the time was propitious for him to renew his father's failed efforts to unite Egypt and Asia and become the greatest ruler on earth—a new Alexander. At this point Antiochus assumed the title *Theos Epiphanes*, which means "God manifest." He actually believed that he was the incarnate manifestation of Zeus. He issued coins purporting to bear the image of the Olympian god, but the picture on the coin was the image of Antiochus. He called himself *Epiphanes*, but the Jews would soon call him *Epimanes*, "a madman."

With the ultimate purpose of uniting Egypt and Syria and quelling the rising tide of Rome, Antiochus planned a war of conquest. In the summer of 169 B.C. he invaded Egypt with a great fleet and a huge force of men, chariots, and elephants. (Although his forces marched through Judea, Antiochus did not attack Jerusalem at this time.) He deposed the young Egyptian king and was on the way to Memphis to become Egypt's new pharaoh when he was met by a Roman ambassador who gave him an ultimatum: either leave Egypt or fight Rome. His forces were too weary to fight Rome, so Antiochus left Egypt and retreated through Judea. It was a humiliating surrender.

Meanwhile a rumor spread that Antiochus had been slain. The Hasideans thought that this was a good time to revolt and put an end to tyranny. Fighting broke out in the streets of Jerusalem. But Antiochus was very much alive and he ordered a massacre. The story is told in 2 Maccabees 5:11-16:

When news of what had happened reached the king, he thought that Judea was in revolt; so he set out from Egypt like a wild beast and took the city by storm. And he ordered his soldiers to cut down without distinction anyone they met and to slay those who took refuge in their houses. Then there was a massacre of young and old, an annihilation of boys, women and children, a slaughter of girls and babies. In no more than three days eighty thousand people were destroyed, forty thousand of them in hand-to-hand encounter, and as many were sold into slavery as were slain. Not content with this, he dared to go into the most holy temple in all the world, guided by Menelaus who had betrayed both the laws and his country; and took the sacred plate in his polluted hands, and with his profane hands he swept away what had been dedicated.

Heinrich Graetz, the prince of Jewish historians, described the massacre as follows:

Having heard of the occurrences in Jerusalem, his [Antiochus Epiphanes'] anger was roused against the Judaeans, and the Covenant of Judaism; his wicked, inhuman nature broke forth against the people. He suddenly attacked Jerusalem, and massacred the inhabitants without regard to age or sex, slaughtering friend and foe alike. He forced his way into the Temple, and entered even the Holy of Holies, and as a mark of contempt for the God who was worshipped there, he removed the golden altar, the candlestick, the table, the golden vessels, and all the treasures which still remained. Menelaus acted as a guide in the spoliation of Israel, whose omnipotence was sung by His followers, but whom he scorned, because He did not interfere with these sacrilegious actions. To palliate both the massacre of innocent people and the desecration of the Temple, he invented a falsehood which long afterwards continued to bring Judaism into bad repute amongst all civilised nations. Antiochus declared that he had seen in the Holy of Holies the statue of a man with a long beard, mounted on an ass, and holding a book in its hand. He believed it to be the statue of the law-giver Moses, who had given the Judaeans inhuman, horrible laws to separate them from all other peoples. Amongst the Greeks and Romans the rumour was spread that Antiochus had found the head of an ass made of gold in the Temple, which the Judaeans venerated, and that consequently they worshipped asses. Antiochus was probably the author of another horrible lie invented to blacken the Judaeans: it was said that he had discovered, lying in bed in the Temple, a Greek, who entreated to be released, as the Judaeans were in the habit of killing a Greek every year, and feeding on his intestines, meanwhile swearing hatred against all Greeks, whom they were determined to destroy. [In later days a similar accusation was made with regard to Christian children.]...

...Antiochus undertook a second campaign against Egypt, and the Judaeans were destined a second time to suffer from his anger....

...He vented his secret anger in unparalleled cruelties upon the Judaeans. They had, he said, shown pleasure at his degradation; they had proclaimed aloud that the god they worshipped humbled the haughty, and had therefore prepared this mortification for him. Apollonius, one of his priestly subjects, and the former governor of Mysia, entered the Judaean capital, accompanied by fierce troops, apparently with peaceful intentions. Suddenly, however, on a Sabbath, when resistance was impossible, the Greek or Macedonian mercenaries threw themselves on the inhabitants, killed men and youths, took women and children prisoners, and sent them to the slave markets.

Apollonius also destroyed many houses in the
capital, and pulled down the walls of Jerusalem, for
he wished it to disappear from the list of important
cities.[14]

It seemed as if God were dead. But God was not dead.
Four hundred years before this event His prophet had
declared, "For he is the living God and he endures forever; his kingdom will not be destroyed, his dominion
will never end. He rescues and he saves; he performs
signs and wonders in the heavens and on the earth. He
has rescued Daniel from the power of the lions" (Daniel
6:26-27). He who "rescued Daniel from the power of the
lions" would also rescue His people from Antiochus
Epiphanes.

But first there would be more persecution. Daniel had
prophesied of Antiochus Epiphanes:

Ships of the western coastlands will oppose him, and
he will lose heart. Then he will turn back and vent
his fury against the holy covenant. He will return
and show favor to those who forsake the holy covenant.

His armed forces will rise up to desecrate the
temple fortress and will abolish the daily sacrifice.
Then they will set up the abomination that causes
desolation (Daniel 11:30-31).

Antiochus determined to put an end not only to Jewish resistance but also to Jewish religion. No longer
would the Torah be the constitution of the Jewish state.
He forbade the use of the Scriptures and the observance of what they taught: the sabbath, circumcision,
food regulations. That was not all. He ordered the immediate adoption of the Greek state religion and
forced the Jews to offer sacrifices in their temple to
the Greek gods. In fact he ordered the sacrifice of the
most unclean of all animals: pigs. Refusal to obey was
punished by death. Synagogues were destroyed, the

sacred Scriptures were burned, and people were slaughtered by the thousands.

In December 168 B.C. the temple of God in Jerusalem was consecrated to the pagan god Zeus. Above the altar was placed a statue of Zeus (it bore an obvious resemblance to Antiochus) and a pig was sacrificed on the altar. This was the "abomination that causes desolation" of Daniel 11:31.

The Hebrew word translated "abomination" is *shigguts,* which means "filthy." *The International Standard Bible Encyclopedia* comments on the prophet's choice of words:

> When Daniel undertook to specify an abomination so surpassingly disgusting to the sense of morality and decency, and so aggressive against everything that was godly as to drive all from its presence and leave its abode desolate, he chose this as the strongest among several synonyms, adding the qualification "that maketh desolate."[15]

Jerusalem was desolate, for only the Greek soldiers and officials, together with the apostate Hellenistic Jews, remained. Antiochus commanded forces to root the Hasideans out and destroy them. But the faithful remnant fled to the mountains around Jerusalem, to the hiding places along the shores of the Dead Sea, and to the wilderness of Judea and carried with them copies of the book of Daniel. As they prepared to war against the Syrian host, they studied the Scriptures and learned that their exile and their suffering would end. They read in Daniel 8:13-14:

> "How long will it take for the vision to be fulfilled— the vision concerning the daily sacrifice, the rebellion that causes desolation, and the surrender of the sanctuary and of the host that will be trampled underfoot?"
>
> He said to me, "It will take 2,300 evenings and mornings; then the sanctuary will be reconsecrated."

The answer to the question "How long?" was "Not long." God was faithful to His promise. Daniel's prophecy was literally fulfilled. Antiochus Epiphanes began his persecution of the Jews in 171 B.C. and exactly 2,300 days later in 165 B.C. the temple was reconsecrated. Graetz wrote of Daniel's prophecy as follows:

> The book of Daniel, with its mystical revelations, was undoubtedly read with great interest by the Assidaeans. The apocalyptic form, which gave each line a peculiar meaning, and reflected the present conditions, lent it a great attraction. Moreover, it solved the problem of the present calamities, and showed the object of the horrible persecutions; these were intended, on the one hand, to destroy sin, and on the other hand, to ennoble believers. It was evident that the duration of the period of affliction had been determined from the beginning, and that this very duration, too, had a secret meaning. The worldly kingdoms would disappear, and at the end time, God's kingdom, the kingdom of the holy ones, would commence, and those who had died or had been slain during the persecutions would awake to eternal life.[16]

The pious Hasideans, strengthened by the Scriptures, became valiant soldiers. Hebrews 11:33-38 speaks of their valor:

> Who through faith conquered kingdoms, administered justice, and gained what was promised; who shut the mouths of lions, quenched the fury of the flames, and escaped the edge of the sword; whose weakness was turned to strength; and who became powerful in battle and routed foreign armies. Women received back their dead, raised to life again. Others were tortured and refused to be released, so that they might gain a better resurrection. Some faced jeers and flogging, while still others were

chained and put in prison. They were stoned; they were sawed in two; they were put to death by the sword. They went about in sheepskins and goatskins, destitute, persecuted and mistreated—the world was not worthy of them.

THE MACCABEES

In 167 B.C. in a little town northeast of Jerusalem a captain in the army of Antiochus Epiphanes erected a pagan altar and commanded the people to come forward and sacrifice a pig in order to demonstrate their loyalty to Antiochus. An aged priest, Mattathias, was ordered to set an example and be the first to obey, but he refused. Then a Judean collaborator approached the altar to sacrifice a pig. Enraged, Mattathias killed the apostate Jew and the Syrian captain. The priest and his five sons destroyed the pagan altar and fled to the mountains around Jerusalem.

The news of Mattathias's rebellion spread quickly. Many who had been timid before, responded when Mattathias and his sons raised their war cry: "Let every one who is zealous for the law and supports the covenant come out with me" (Apocrypha, 1 Maccabees 2:27). At first it was guerrilla warfare and the cause of the rebels seemed hopeless. First Maccabees 2:29-38 describes the situation:

> Then many seekers for uprightness and justice went down into the wilderness to settle, with their sons and their wives and their cattle, because their hardships had become so severe. And news reached the king's agents and the forces that were in Jerusalem, in the City of David, that men who had disregarded the king's order had gone down to the hiding-places in the wilderness. And they pursued them in force and overtook them, and pitched their camp against them and prepared to attack them on the sabbath day. And they said to them, "Enough!

Come out and do as the king commands, and you
will live." And they said, "We will not come out nor
do as the king commands, and break the sabbath."
Then they hastened to attack them. And they made
no response to them; they did not throw a stone at
them nor block up their hiding-places, for they said,
"Let us all die guiltless. We call heaven and earth to
witness that you destroy us unlawfully." So they
attacked them on the sabbath, and they died, with
their wives and their children and their cattle, to a
number of a thousand people."

Mattathias decided that the policy of letting the Greeks
massacre them on the sabbath was wrong; from that time
on the Jews could defend themselves on the sabbath day.
This decision was the turning point in the war. Antiochus
soon learned that he had a violent rebellion on his hands.

Mattathias died within a year of his tearing down of
the pagan altar. On his deathbed he appointed his son
Judah (also known as Judas), who was surnamed Maccabeus, as commander-in-chief. Some scholars explain that
the name *Maccabeus* is an acrostic consisting of the first
syllables of the Maccabees' war cry, *"Mi-ko-mocho ba-eilem?"*
which means, "Who is like unto Thee, O Lord?" Other
scholars say his name is derived from *makkebet*, the Hebrew word for "hammer."

The appointment of Judah was a wise choice. God
greatly used him in humbling Antiochus Epiphanes.

At first Judah Maccabeus and his men made sporadic
attacks against unguarded cities. But as his forces grew
bolder, he gradually began to attack the outposts of the
Syrian forces. The Syrian commanders deployed battal-
ions of Syrian soldiers and Hellenized Jews, and many
times it seemed as if the rebels were cornered. But before each battle the Maccabees fasted and prayed, and
the Lord brought them through victorious.

Never before in military history were so many defeated
by so few. Antiochus realized that he had a full-blown

rebellion on his hands, one that had to be quickly suppressed. So he appointed his ablest general, Lysias, to wipe out all vestiges of Judaism. Lysias led an elite army and was so confident of victory that he announced beforehand the price he would charge for the Jewish slaves he would capture!

Judah and his men gathered at Mizpeh, where centuries before, Samuel had called the people of Israel to repentance (1 Samuel 7:5). There the Maccabees prayed and God answered their prayer. That night the brilliant General Lysias decided to divide his troops and send a contingent of cavalry and infantry to make a surprise attack against the Jewish forces in the morning. But Judah "got wind of it" and during the night he and his men broke camp and moved on (Apocrypha, 1 Maccabees 4:3). The next morning Lysias's fighting troops found nobody at Judah's camp, and while they searched the mountains, the Jews utterly routed the remainder of the Syrian army.

The road to Jerusalem was now open. With songs of praise *(Hallelu Yah)* on their lips, the Maccabean army entered the city, which had been desecrated three years ago. There the soldiers dropped their swords so that they could finish what they had been fighting for: the cleansing of the temple.

According to 1 Maccabees 4:36, "Judas and his brothers said, 'Now that our enemies have been defeated, let us go up to purify the sanctuary and dedicate it.'" The victors removed every vestige of paganism and erected a new altar. On the 25th day of Kislev (usually in December), exactly three years after the abomination of desolation, the temple was rededicated.

To celebrate the rededication, the Jews feasted for eight days. This celebration was the origin of Hanukkah. Almost two centuries later our Lord commemorated it: "Then came the Feast of Dedication at Jerusalem. It was winter, and Jesus was in the temple area walking in Solomon's Colonnade" (John 10:22-23).

A beautiful tradition based on a legend arose in connection with Hanukkah. The tradition is the lighting of the menorah (candlestick). According to the legend, at the time of the rededication there was just enough oil to keep the "eternal" light of the menorah in the temple burning for one day and it would take eight days for the priest to prepare more oil that was untouched by pagan hands. But a miracle happened and the single cruse of oil lasted and the menorah was kept lawfully lighted while more oil was being prepared.

The legend is fascinating, but the real miracle is that once more God preserved His people so that He could fulfill His promise to Abraham that "all peoples on earth will be blessed through you" (Genesis 12:3).

5

The Hasmonean Dynasty

THE YOKE OF THE GENTILES BROKEN

The title *Hasmonean* was first used of the Maccabees by Josephus in his *Antiquities of the Jews.*[1] Its etymology is uncertain. Perhaps Josephus coined the title from the name of the great-grandfather of Mattathias: Asamonaios. Some have attempted to connect the title with Heshmon mentioned in Joshua 15:27 or with Hushim mentioned in 1 Chronicles 8:11. Others have tried to identify the title *Hasmonean* with Hashmonah mentioned in Numbers 33:29-30. One of the problems confronting etymologists is that the name *Hasmonean* is never used in the books of the Maccabees as a title for the Maccabeus family and their successors. However, the name is used in the Talmud as the title for the Maccabees and their descendants (see Middoth 1:6 and Shabbath 21b). The *Encyclopedia Judaica* states:

> The Hasmoneans were a priestly family, probably one of those which had moved from the territory of Benjamin to the lowlands of Lydda in the last days of the First Temple. They belonged to the Jehoiarib division of priests, who lived in Modi'in on the border of Samaria and Judea. When the restrictive edicts of Antiochus were extended to the

country towns and villages of Jewish Palestine, Mattathias b. Johanan, then the head of the family, raised the banner of revolt in Modi'in, uniting under his leadership all those who were opposed to Antiochus's policy.[2]

After the death of Mattathias b. Johanan in 167/166 B.C. the leadership of the Hasmoneans fell, as we have seen, to his son Judah Maccabeus. It was Judah who scored many military victories against the armies of Antiochus and the Seleucid empire and made the title *Hasmonean* feared, respected, and also hated among the Jews and their enemies.

When Judah Maccabeus and his men rededicated the temple in 165 B.C., some of them thought they had attained their goal. But internal factions soon made them realize they were facing insurmountable problems. For example the Hasidim, who were the nucleus of what later became the sect of the Pharisees, became disenchanted with the Hasmonean leadership and wanted more of a voice within the emerging and struggling dynasty. The Hasidim withdrew their support of the Hasmoneans in 162 B.C.

Another problem that the Maccabees faced in their war with Antiochus Epiphanes was the fact that Judea's neighboring nations, whenever they could, gladly helped the Syrians fight against the Jews. In fact Judea's neighbors used the same tactics back then that the Arab nations of the twentieth century are using with modern Israel. The surrounding countries not only helped Syria fight against the Jews by sending soldiers and money; they also persecuted the Jews who lived in their midst. The pagans of Jaffa, for instance, drowned two hundred Jewish men, women, and children who lived among them. Judah sent punitive expeditions against the offending nations.

Meanwhile things were going badly for Antiochus in the East. In the summer of 164 B.C. he was stricken with a loathsome malady that affected his mind and when he learned that Jerusalem and the temple were in Jewish hands, he went mad. Before his death he wrote a letter appointing his nine-year-old son Antiochus V as his successor.

Judah's old enemy Lysias believed that now at last he could avenge his defeat at Mizpeh. He appointed himself viceroy for the new king and raised a huge army of mercenaries from all of the enemies that surrounded Judea. The most formidable army that the Maccabees ever faced, it included a group of thirty-two trained elephants. Josephus described the battle as follows:

> So the king took this army, and marched hastily out of Antioch, with Lysias, who had the command of the whole, and came to Idumea, and thence went up to the city Bethsura, a city that was strong, and not to be taken without great difficulty. He set about this city, and besieged it. And while the inhabitants of Bethsura courageously opposed him, and sallied out upon him, and burnt his engines of war, a great deal of time was spent in the siege. But when Judas heard of the king's coming, he raised the siege of the citadel, and met the king, and pitched his camp in certain straits, at a place called Bethzachariah, at the distance of seventy furlongs from the enemy; but the king soon drew his forces from Bethsura, and brought them to those straits. And as soon as it was day, he put his men in battle-array, and made his elephants follow one another through the narrow passes, because they could not be set sideways by one another. Now round about every elephant there were a thousand footmen, and five hundred horsemen. The elephants also had high towers [upon their backs], and archers [in them]. And he also made the rest of his army to go up the mountains, and put his friends before the rest; and gave orders for the army to shout aloud, and so he attacked the enemy. He also exposed to sight their

golden and brazen shields, so that a glorious splendour was sent from them; and when they shouted the mountains echoed again. When Judas saw this, he was not terrified, but received the enemy with great courage, and slew about six hundred of the first ranks.[3]

It was during this battle that Judah's younger brother Eleazar saw an elephant that was larger than the others and was arrayed with gorgeous gaudy adornments. Guessing that this elephant was carrying the boy-king in its wooden tower, Eleazar attacked the troops that were defending the elephant, ran beneath it, and stabbed its belly. The huge animal fell dead on Eleazar and crushed him to death. It was a futile gesture: Antiochus V was not riding that elephant and the death of one elephant did not slow the relentless advance of the Syrians.

Judah and his army fled to Jerusalem and Lysias laid siege to Jerusalem. The siege lasted for months. It was a sabbatical year during which the Jews could not, according to the law, cultivate a new crop, and so it seemed as if at last the Syrians would starve the Jews into surrendering.

Lysias, however, received some bad news from home: his rival, Philip, was the legal regent to Antiochus V. Philip had advanced from the East and occupied Antioch, and Lysias realized that he must return to Syria. He proposed a truce with the Jews. There were two issues to be negotiated: religious liberty and political independence. The Syrians offered to yield the first if the Jews would give up their struggle for political freedom. There was a temporary truce, although neither side had any real intention of keeping the peace. Judah wanted political as well as religious freedom and Lysias would return after he took care of his rival.

Judah Maccabeus, who proved himself to be a capable general, was succeeded by his brother Jonathan, who led the people for seventeen years. He was not the military leader that Judah was, nor was he a statesman. Actually he was a politician and his successes were due mainly to the skill with which he played one man against another. He was thoroughly unscrupulous.

In 152 B.C. a civil war erupted in Syria. Both sides were eager for Jonathan's support. By manipulating both sides, Jonathan obtained appointments as high priest, governor of Judea, and general. He entered Jerusalem in triumph, rebuilt the city, and fortified the temple area.

In 143 B.C. Jonathan was lured into a trap by Trypho and was slain.[4] When Jonathan died, there was only one son of Mattathias left: the aging but valiant Simon, who was noted for his wisdom. Simon gathered an "assembly of the great." (Later the Sanhedrin claimed to have developed from this assembly.) During this assembly Simon was appointed hereditary ruler and high priest "until a true prophet shall rise."[5] Although Simon was never anointed king, he is generally regarded as the founder of the Hasmonean dynasty.

Simon, like his brothers, would suffer a violent death, but before he died he was able to negotiate political independence for the Jews. In 142 B.C. the yoke of the Gentiles was removed from Israel and people began to write in their documents and contracts, "In the first year of Simon the great high priest and commander and leader of the Jews" (Apocrypha, 1 Maccabees 15:6). After 450 years Jerusalem was once more the capital of a sovereign state.

For a few short years Jerusalem actually became the "city of peace," as its name implies. Commercial relations were established and Jewish slaves were redeemed. It seems that the author of 1 Maccabees actually believed that prophecies in Isaiah and Micah had been fulfilled as he described the "new" Jerusalem:

> [The Jews] tilled the land in peace, and the land gave her increase, and the trees of the plains their fruit. The old men sat in the streets, they talked together of the common good, and the young men put on glorious and fine apparel. Every man sat

under his own vine and his fig tree, and there was none to frighten them (Apocrypha, 1 Maccabees 14:41). (See Isaiah 2:2-4; Micah 4:1-4).

THE FRIENDSHIP OF ROME SOUGHT

This newly won utopia was not paradise regained. Subtle changes had taken place in Israel after Mattathias's death, especially in the attitudes of the new Jewish leadership. For instance, Mattathias had begun the revolution against Antiochus Epiphanes by rallying the Jewish people with the challenge, "Let every one who is zealous for the law and supports the convenant come out with me" (Apocrypha, 1 Maccabees 2:27). His appeal was to the Law and the Prophets. Under the leadership of Judah Maccabeus the emphasis changed from Scripture to diplomacy.

The Diplomacy of Judah Maccabeus

Judah entered into what he thought was a mutual defense pact with Rome. Little did he know that Rome never defended any nation and within eighty years the bitterly won independence of the Jews would be trodden under the feet of Pompey's armies. Judea would learn of a despot who was even more cruel than Antiochus Epiphanes.

How could Judea's leader have signed such a treaty? Judah Maccabeus, himself a brilliant general, had become enamored of the military prowess of Rome. Josephus said of Judah:

> Who hearing of the power of the Romans, and that they had conquered in war Galatia, and Iberia, and Carthage, and Libya; and that, besides these, they had subdued Greece, and their kings, Perseus, and Philip, and Antiochus the Great also; he resolved to enter into a league of friendship with them. He therefore sent to Rome some of his friends....They also made a decree... engraven in brass. The decree

itself was this: "The decree of the senate concerning a league of assistance and friendship with the nation of the Jews. It shall not be lawful for any that are subject to the Romans to make war with the nation of the Jews, nor to assist those that do so, either by sending them corn, or ships, or money; and if any attack be made upon the Jews, the Romans shall assist them, as far as they are able; and again, if any attack be made upon the Romans, the Jews shall assist them."[6]

The treaty signed with Rome was engraved in brass. The brass itself had value, but the treaty was worthless because Rome never had any intention of sending help to the Jews. Rome was only waiting to destroy the Syrian empire before sending its hordes to march through the streets of Jerusalem.

Not only was the treaty worthless; it put Israel in a terrible position, for from that day forward the Jewish nation had to look to Rome to solve their problems. The Romans, of course, solved all their problems with Roman "justice," which meant that what was good for Rome was good for all.

Thus through diplomacy and desire for friendship with Rome, the new leadership yielded up the nation's freedom to follow the Scriptures and serve the Lord as a politically free people.

Jonathan's Lust for Power

There was another difference after Mattathias's death. As great as the Maccabees were in leading the Jewish state to freedom, they soon exhibited their own lust for power by actively seeking and accepting political access to the office of high priest for themselves and their posterity. As a result the high priesthood stayed under regal control. This development reflected disregard of a central truth of Judaism: The high priest does not represent the king; he represents God. As Hebrews 5:4 says of the high priest, "No one takes this honor upon himself; he must be called by God."

The entrance of the Maccabees into the high priesthood involves the story of an impostor: In 152 B.C. a young man conquered Ptolemais, which was a seaport of Syria. He claimed to be Alexander Epiphanes, the younger son of Antiochus Epiphanes. According to 1 Maccabees 10:1-2, "Alexander Epiphanes, the son of Antiochus, went up and took possession of Ptolemais; and they received him and he reigned there." Today, however, most historians concede that this Alexander Epiphanes was actually an impostor whose real name was Alexander Balas.

All of Syria's neighbors wanted her to have a puppet ruler who was generally held in contempt so Attalus II, king of Pergamum, "discovered" Alexander, evidently because he looked like Antiochus Epiphanes. Attalus declared that Balas was in fact the son of the late king of Syria, Antiochus Epiphanes. In Rome the senate, as eager as Attalus to have a weakling puppet on the Syrian throne, also recognized Balas as the heir to the throne.

Meanwhile in Israel, Jonathan had succeeded Judah Maccabeus as ruler. Now Jonathan and Alexander Balas had something in common: they both wanted to be friends of Rome. Josephus recorded a letter written by Alexander to Jonathan:

> King Alexander to his brother Jonathan, sendeth greeting. We have long ago heard of thy courage and thy fidelity, and for that reason have sent to thee, to make with thee a league of friendship and mutual assistance. We therefore do ordain thee this day the high priest of the Jews, and that thou beest called my friend. I have also sent thee, as presents, a purple robe and a golden crown, and desire that, now thou art by us honoured, thou wilt in like manner respect us also.[7]

Appointing Jonathan as high priest was a brilliant stroke on the part of Balas, as it played into Jonathan's secret ambition for power. Josephus wrote, "When Jonathan had received this letter, he put on the pontifical robe at the time of the feast of tabernacles, four years after the death of his brother Judah, for at that time no high priest had been made."[8]

Antiochus Epiphanes had begun his attempt to destroy the Jewish religion by deposing the rightful high priest and appointing a man of his own choice. This act had led to the Maccabean revolt and now one of the sons of Mattathias was eagerly accepting the high priesthood from an impostor whose very ability to bestow this honor was based on his claim to be the son of Antiochus Epiphanes!

Many students of history claim that Jonathan was a clever diplomat—that he accomplished by diplomacy what he could not accomplish by arms. Actually his acceptance of the high priesthood from a contemptible usurper was an act of great folly, legitimizing the regal control of the priesthood. From this time on until the Romans destroyed the temple (and the high priesthood) in A.D. 70, whoever ruled Jerusalem also controlled the office of the high priest. This proved to be a far greater disaster for the Jews than even the Babylonian captivity.

Max I. Dimont reminded us of the famous limerick:

> There was a young lady of Niger
> Who smiled as she rode on a tiger;
> They came back from the ride
> With the lady inside
> And the smile on the face of the tiger.[9]

For a while the Jewish nation enjoyed political freedom, although its leaders were smiling at the Roman tiger. Then its leaders took a ride on the tiger's back by signing the treaty of friendship. The Roman tiger simply swallowed up its Jewish "friend," but it was the lust for power of Israel's leaders that really caused its downfall.

6

The Jewish Nation under Rome

When the Maccabees finally defeated the Syrians, Judea was once more an independent, self-governing nation for the first time since the Babylonian captivity. The fierce struggle to defend its right to worship God according to the Scriptures had also won the nation of Israel its political freedom. This victory was a critical juncture in Jewish history.

By the time Judea won its liberty in 143 B.C., 70 percent of the Jews of the world lived in nations that had been conquered by Rome. Rome had already begun to domineer the earth.

We now turn very briefly to the Jews scattered in the Roman world in the first centuries B.C. and A.D. As we continue to recount intertestamental history, New Testament readers will recognize more and more familiar names and places and will become excited as they see how God was preparing His people—in Judea and throughout the world—for the coming of His Son.

THE DIASPORA UNDER ROME

Jewish history is not just the annals of a people in a land; it is the story of a diaspora, a scattering that has lasted until now (over 2,500 years). Nebuchadnezzar thought that the Jews he deported to Babylon would be assimilated among his peoples and disappear as a nation from the face of the earth, thus demonstrating the impotence of Jehovah. But the God of Abraham is not impotent; He is all-powerful! Nebuchadnezzar lived to testify: "I praised the Most High; I honored and glorified him who lives forever. His dominion is an eternal dominion; his kingdom endures from generation to generation" (Daniel 4:34).

Proud Nebuchadnezzar destroyed the temple, but the Lord of the temple destroyed him. All Nebuchadnezzar did was help the Lord fulfill His promise to Abraham: "I will make you into a great nation and I will bless you; I will make your name great, and you will be a blessing. I will bless those who bless you, and whoever curses you I will curse; and all peoples on earth will be blessed through you" (Genesis 12:2-3). Nebuchadnezzar scattered the Jews all over the Babylonian empire so that in the fullness of time "all peoples on earth" would be blessed through the offspring of Abraham. The great commission inherent in the Abrahamic covenant was to be fulfilled "first for the Jew, then for the Gentile" (Romans 1:16).

The New Testament gives us history's best synopsis of the extent of Jewish communities in the Roman empire in the intertestamental period. Acts 2:5 tells us that on the day of Pentecost "there were staying in Jerusalem God-fearing Jews from every nation under heaven" and verses 9-11 list some of the places these men had traveled from. From the East there were Parthians, Medes, and Elamites; from the North and Northwest had come residents of Cappadocia, Pontus, Phrygia, and Pamphylia; from the West there were men of Mediterranean countries such as Egypt, Libya, Crete, and Rome; and from the South had come inhabitants of Arabia. This list is by no means complete. Neither Greece nor Syria is mentioned, although they had large populations of Jews, many of whom must have celebrated Pentecost in Jerusalem.

The history of these Jewish communities is not germane

to our theme. What is important is that wherever ten or more observant male Jews lived, they built synagogues. Because of the diaspora, synagogues were built all over the world.

Synagogues

The synagogue is one of the most important factors of Jewish survival. The *Encyclopedia Judaica* states:

> There are almost no historical dates concerning its origin. As its birth is lost in the mists of antiquity and apparently took place unheralded, so it grew to maturity in conditions of obscurity, and makes its definite appearance about the first century of the Christian era as a fully grown and firmly established institution. There is, however, an almost universal consensus of opinion as to the place and origin of its birth.[1]

As we have seen, when the Jews were driven into the Babylonian captivity, they knew that it was God's punishment. They had broken the law, worshiped idols, stoned the prophets, and neglected the sabbath. At last they realized that God means what He says and in Babylon the Jews started to change. They studied and obeyed the Law and the Prophets. They gathered on the sabbath to read the Scriptures and started to apply them to their lives. They turned from idolatry, and God put iron in their spines to follow Him and His Word.

The small fellowship meetings first started in homes, but as increasing numbers of Jews attended, they realized they needed separate places of worship. Thus they started building synagogues.

Converts

Throughout the centuries, wherever they migrated, the Jews built synagogues. During the Roman conquest, synagogues became islands of praise to Jehovah in a morass of the vilest abominations imaginable.

These vile excesses disgusted thoughtful Gentiles and the synagogues seemed like lighthouses to them. The Jews, who had business dealings with these Gentiles, invited them to the synagogues, where Greek translations of the Scriptures were read. As a result many Gentiles converted to Judaism.

Meanwhile in Judea a strong religious party was becoming dominant: the Pharisees. They were almost fanatically evangelistic, as our Lord recognized: "You travel over land and sea to win a single convert" (Matthew 23:15). And the Pharisees were successful.

But it was not easy for a Gentile to convert to Judaism, for one of the requirements was circumcision. This ritual was very painful for adults and extremely humiliating. Nevertheless many Gentiles were converted during the first century B.C.

Besides the actual converts, many more Gentiles intellectually accepted the truths of Judaism, regularly attended a synagogue, and believed the Scriptures. They were called "hearers of the Law."

Thus in most synagogues there were three kinds of worshipers: Jews, Gentiles who had converted to Judaism, and Gentiles who were "hearers of the Law." God was bringing Gentiles into the synagogues in preparation for the fulfilling of His promise that all peoples on earth would be blessed through the Jews.

In the book of Acts we read that wherever Paul went, he preached the gospel in the synagogue first—to both Jews and Gentiles. For example Paul's first recorded message in Pisidian Antioch was given in the local synagogue and he addressed it to "men of Israel and you Gentiles who worship God" (Acts 13:16). Acts 14:1 tells us: "At Iconium Paul and Barnabas went as usual into the Jewish synagogue. There they spoke so effectively that a great number of Jews and Gentiles believed." At Thessalonica Paul preached in the synagogue on three consecutive sabbaths and "some of the Jews were persuaded and joined

Paul and Silas, as did a large number of God- fearing Greeks and not a few prominent women" (Acts 17:4). In Christ the "God-fearing Greeks" ("hearers of the Law") did not have to undergo the rite of circumcision.

Paul was the apostle to the Gentiles, but wherever he traveled, he first went to the synagogue. He was not forsaking his calling; his method was clear. In the synagogues he could preach to both Jews and Gentiles. This was his strategy for bringing the gospel to all men everywhere.

At Athens Paul started out as usual: "He was greatly distressed to see that the city was full of idols. So he reasoned in the synagogue with the Jews and the God-fearing Greeks" (Acts 17:16-17). Then he tried philosophical discussions on Mars Hill, but unfortunately this new method was not visibly successful. Paul founded no church in Athens.

THE DECLINE OF THE HASMONEANS

Simon Maccabeus was killed in 135 B.C. The generation that had successfully fought the Syrian armies of Antiochus Epiphanes was dying out. The new generation was proud of its military victories and hoped for even greater success, but thirsting after power and glory, they forgot that their struggle began for religious, not political reasons. Paul Johnson wrote:

> The recreation of the state and kingdom, originally and ostensibly on a basis of pure religious fundamentalism—the defense of the faith—revived all the inherent problems of the earlier monarchy, and in particular the irresolvable conflict between the aims and methods of the state and the nature of the Jewish religion.
>
> This conflict is reflected in the personal history of the Hasmoneans themselves, and the story of their rise and fall is a memorable study in hubris. They began as the avengers of martyrs; they ended as religious oppressors themselves. They came to

power at the head of an eager guerrilla band; they ended surrounded by mercenaries. Their kingdom, founded in faith, dissolved in impiety.[2]

John Hyrcanus I

Simon Maccabeus was replaced by his son John Hyrcanus I as leader of the Hasmoneans. We will see how under his leadership the oppressed became the oppressors.

During the early years of his reign (134–104 B.C.) the new Judean commonwealth had some features of a miniature golden age. George Foot Moore wrote:

> Triumphant Judaism was under no temptation to assimilate itself to the religions of the heathen over whom its God had given it the victory. Some enthusiasts saw in events of the time the Lord's deliverance foretold in ancient prophecies and the dawning of the yet more glorious day that was to follow. The Jews in other lands shared in this exaltation of spirit.
>
> As in older times, the triumphs of the Lord were a revival of religion, in the sense, at least, of enthusiasm for it and heightened loyalty to it.[3]

Josephus said of Hyrcanus: "He was esteemed by God worthy of three of the greatest privileges—the government of his nation, the dignity of the high priesthood, and prophecy; for God was with him, and enabled him to know futurities [to know and foretell the future]."[4] But Josephus was wrong. Hyrcanus was not worthy of the government of his nation because he was not a son of David. He should never have been high priest because he was not a son of Aaron. Nor did God enable him to foretell the future, as we shall see.

In winning their war for independence, the Jews surrendered the most significant gain of their revolt against Syria, for once more the king became the high priest. This designation was abhorrent to the mass of the people and contrary to the letter and spirit of the Scriptures. In accepting the high priesthood, Hyrcanus was approving the principle Antiochus Epiphanes wanted to institute: the king is in charge of the temple.

The reign of John Hyrcanus I is associated with a war to recapture the territory that had been part of Israel in the time of David and Solomon. The Jews actually fought three wars in the intertestamental period. The first was for religious freedom. Their victory then is still celebrated each December at Hanukkah. In the second war the victorious Hasmoneans cleverly took advantage of the growing power of Rome and manipulated it to win political independence from Syria. Judea became a friend of Rome, but Rome would soon prove that it had only one friend: Rome. The third war was for the reconquest of the ancient land of Israel as it was before the kingdom was divided. This was John Hyrcanus's goal.

Perhaps we can best understand Hyrcanus by thinking of him as a prototype Zionist. In the Torah, which Hyrcanus's father and grandfather had defended, God had promised Abraham, "All the land that you see I will give to you and your offspring forever" (Genesis 13:15). Hyrcanus believed this, but he also believed that it would be convenient for Rome to help God protect His land from Syria. Thus one of the first things Hyrcanus did was to renew the treaties that Judah and Simon Maccabeus had made with Rome.

If Hyrcanus could have foretold the future, he would have known that Roman hordes would march into Jerusalem, that Pompey would violate the holy of holies, and that a century of untold cruelty to the Jewish people would be climaxed by the destruction of the temple. He would have known that all of this would happen as a direct result of the alliances he, his father, and his uncle had made with Rome.

In his zeal to recapture the land, Hyrcanus was quick to institute a policy of territorial expansion. He wanted to restore Judea to the limits it enjoyed under David and

Solomon. Hyrcanus realized that to achieve his goal he needed to gain control of the trade routes. The seaports on the Mediterranean as well as the land routes were all controlled by pagan cities.

By this time the people were tired of fighting, and warfare was expensive, but these drawbacks did not deter Hyrcanus. He was quite resourceful in dealing with both problems. According to Josephus, he "opened the sepulchre of David, who excelled all other kings in riches, and took out of it three thousand talents. He was also the first of the Jews that, relying on this wealth, maintained foreign troops."[5]

Fifty years earlier Antiochus Epiphanes had kindled the wrath of the Maccabees and the entire Jewish nation when he replaced a high priest who would not raid the treasury with one who would. Now, in John Hyrcanus, the Jews had another high priest who would. He was willing to violate the principles for which his father, his four uncles, and his grandfather had given their lives.

Perhaps Hyrcanus thought of himself as a second Joshua who was commissioned not only to conquer the land, but also to destroy the Canaanites, for he oppressed the people of the lands he conquered—particularly Idumea and Samaria.

To the south he warred against the Idumeans, since one of the main trade routes between Egypt and Asia passed through Idumea. Hyrcanus subdued the Idumeans and compelled them to convert to Judaism and be circumcised. This terrible act was to have a terrifying result, for among the Idumeans "converted" to Judaism was the grandfather of Herod the Great. As Solomon Zeitlin explained: "According to the view of the Pharisees, a person whose ancestors were proselytes was a Judaean of equal religious status with a native of ancient lineage. Only the Sadducees held otherwise."[6] When Hyrcanus forcibly circumcised Herod's grandfather, he gave legitimacy to Herod's claim as king of the Jews. Herod was the greatest oppressor in Jewish history.

North of Jerusalem the Samaritans had built a temple

on mount Gerizim. Hyrcanus had no intention of permitting a rival temple, so he captured the whole of Samaria and destroyed their temple in 107 B.C.

H. L. Ellison commented:

> This was not simply an act of spite. Even as he had earlier forced the Idumeans to accept Judaism, so now he was forcing the Samaritans to conform to Jerusalem's version of Judaism.
>
> When the Samaritans were freed from Jewish rule by the coming of the Romans, there remained a legacy of bitterness that could not be bridged. So while in one sense the Samaritan schism began with the return of the Jews from exile, in another it was made unhealable by the action of John Hyrcanus.
>
> For the Jews it was not the Temple as such that mattered. There is no evidence that they felt very strongly about the strange sanctuary at Elephantine, or the later copy of the Jerusalem Temple at Leontopolis in Egypt.
>
> What mattered was the Samaritans' proud, defiant claim that this was a holy place chosen by God (Jn. 4:20), that they had an Aaronic priesthood superior to the Hasmoneans, who took over the office in Jerusalem in the middle of the second century [B.C.], and that they interpreted the Law according to an older tradition—so they claimed—than that in force in Jerusalem.
>
> In many points it seems to have been stricter than that of the Pharisees, as was indeed also that of the Sadducees.[7]

During the next two generations the Samaritans chafed under the Hasmonean dynasty. Only the Roman conquest of Judea freed them from their suppression. Then the Samaritans prospered—not because the Romans were altruistic, but because they were using the Samaritans to punish the Jews. In A.D. 135 after the Bar Kokhba revolution, the Samaritans were permitted to rebuild their temple on mount Gerizim. Thus the punishment of the Jews continued.

The Pharisees

Early in his reign Hyrcanus was a disciple of the Pharisees and was highly esteemed by them. Josephus wrote:

> Now Hyrcanus was a disciple of theirs [the Pharisees], and greatly beloved by them. And when he once invited them to a feast, and entertained them very kindly, when he saw them in a good humour, he began to say to them, that they knew he was desirous to a righteous man, and to do all things whereby he might please God, which was the profession of the Pharisees also.
>
> However, he desired, that if they observed him offending in any point, and going out of the right way, they would call him back and correct him.[8]

According to Jewish tradition, Hyrcanus was vouchsafed the offices of high priest, prophet, and ruler of Judea and was the only one to attain all three.[9] He was stunned when one of the Pharisees (Eleazar) advised him to lay down the high priesthood and content himself with the civil government. When Hyrcanus asked Eleazar why he should give up the high priesthood, he was told: "Thy mother had been a captive under the reign of Antiochus Epiphanes."[10] This was a lie being told by the enemies of Hyrcanus in their attempt to disqualify him from being the high priest. Hyrancus, furious and insulted by this false allegation, took steps to censor the authority, power, and public traditions of the Pharisees. This censorship infuriated the Pharisees, who in turn censored Hyrcanus. The fact that Hyrcanus's administration had by this time become more secular and less concerned with established religious traditions gave more ammunition to the Pharisees. As the rift deepened between Hyrcanus and the Pharisees, Hyrcanus aligned himself with the Sadducees. "Jonathan [Hyrcanus] officiated in the high priesthood for 80 years and in the end became a Sadducee."[11]

The change from Pharisee to Sadducee was not a mere move from the Whigs to the Tories. Hyrcanus's refusal to give up the high priesthood and his decision to join the wealthy, secular Sadducees made it apparent to the religious Jews and the Pharisees that the high priesthood could be bought and sold—and from this time on Jewish history indicates that the high priesthood could definitely be had for a price!

Webster's New International Unabridged Dictionary (second edition) defines the word *pharisaical* as "resembling the Pharisees, addicted to external forms and ceremonies; outwardly but not inwardly religious; formal; hypocritical; self-righteous."

There is much misunderstanding about the Pharisees. It is true that John the Baptist called some of the Pharisees of his day a "brood of vipers" (Matthew 3:7) and that our Lord called them "hypocrites" (Mark 7:1-7). But some of the Pharisees—such as Gamaliel, the teacher of Paul—are among the most noble scholars of Jewish history.

Josephus described the Pharisees as "a body of Jews who profess to be more religious than the rest and to explain the laws more precisely."[12] This group of Jews set very high standards for themselves and for the people. Some of the Pharisees lived up to these standards, and some did not. We can never understand Jewish history or the Jewish people if we always equate a Pharisee with hypocrisy. The Jewish leaders themselves were well aware of the sore spots and plagues of the Pharisaic party in their midst.

Most conservative Christian scholars believe that the Pharisees originally were the *Hasidim* (literally "the pious"), who initially rebelled against Antiochus Epiphanes. They are called the Hasideans in the book of the Maccabees. The record is not clear, but it seems that the Hasidim fought only for religious freedom. When the Hasmoneans fought for political freedom, the Hasidim did not join them. The Hasidim believed in the Law and the Prophets and were convinced that they were the spiritual successors to Ezra, who expounded the Scriptures (Nehemiah 8:8).

Ezra did what every pastor does each Lord's day, but the Pharisees claimed that as they expounded the Scriptures, God's oral law was being proclaimed. They believed that along with the Scriptures, God had revealed to Moses an unwritten tradition that explained and supplemented the laws in the Pentateuch. It was on this point that our Lord disagreed with the Pharisees. Jesus said to them, "You have a fine way of setting aside the commands of God in order to observe your own traditions!" (Mark 7:9)

The Pharisees called the oral law "the tradition of the elders" (Mark 7:5). We strongly disagree with the Pharisees concerning its validity, but we are grateful that they nourished the best aspects of Judaism. They kept alive

1. their belief in the coming of the Messiah;
2. their belief in one God;
3. their teaching on the future life (the Greeks taught a resurrection of the soul, but the Pharisees emphasized the resurrection of the body);
4. their doctrine of retribution and rewards.

The Pharisees can also be credited with upholding personal religion—inculcating the sense of sin and the need of repentance, grace, and forgiveness. That they were responsible for the institution of the synagogue and its worship is very doubtful, but it is certain that they fostered and developed the synagogue liturgy and thereby spread the concept of spiritual worship. William Oesterley wrote:

> In later days, as we learn from the Gospels, there was a certain falling away from the high ideals of earlier times. That is the way of humanity; but we have been concerned here only with the Pharisees

during the century or so immediately following the time when they appeared as the spiritual descendants of the *Chasidim.*[13]

The Pharisees desired more than independence. They wanted a nation under God—a nation obeying His precepts. Thus they challenged the high priesthood of John Hyrcanus I. Hyrcanus wanted something else and he got it.

The Sadducees

There is also much misunderstanding concerning the Sadducees. According to the New Testament (Matthew 22:23; Mark 12:18; Luke 20:27) they denied the doctrine of the resurrection of the body. Because many liberal modern theologians also deny this truth, many casual readers of the New Testament equate the Sadducees with today's liberal theologians. This is simply a bad analogy.

Actually the Sadducees were rigid traditionalists! They accepted the Torah and nothing else as God's revealed and valid law. Therefore they rejected the Pharisees' oral law. The Sadducees rejected the resurrection of the body because they did not see the doctrine in the Law of Moses.

Understanding their adherence to the written Law, one can better appreciate their utter consternation when our Lord answered their tricky question in Luke 20:27-40:

> Some of the Sadducees, who say there is no resurrection, came to Jesus with a question. "Teacher," they said, "Moses wrote for us that if a man's brother dies and leaves a wife but no children, the man must marry the widow and have children for his brother. Now there were seven brothers. The first one married a woman and died childless. The second and then the third married her, and in the same way the seven died, leaving no children. Finally, the woman died too. Now then, at the resurrection whose wife will she be, since the seven were married to her?"

Jesus replied, "The people of this age marry and are given in marriage. But those who are considered worthy of taking part in that age and in the resurrection from the dead will neither marry nor be given in marriage, and they can no longer die; for they are like the angels. They are God's children, since they are children of the resurrection. But in the account of the bush, even Moses showed that the dead rise, for he calls the Lord 'the God of Abraham, and the God of Isaac, and the God of Jacob.' He is not the God of the dead, but of the living, for to him are all alive."

Some of the teachers of the law responded, "Well said, teacher!" And no one dared to ask him any more questions.

The Lord tore down the very foundation of the Sadducees' argument. Moses in the Law did teach the resurrection of the body.

While the Sadducees were rigid formalists in their religious beliefs, they found it profitable to oppose the Pharisees religiously and politically. The Sadducees became the intermediaries between the priests and the rulers. Thus when John Hyrcanus became a friend of Rome and later a Sadducee, he created a social and political climate that would eventually climax in the destruction of Jerusalem.

The treaty Hyrcanus made with Rome was hailed as a great diplomatic achievement. However within a few decades Judea's new friend would come to dinner and expel the host! Rome would station its soldiers in Judea and from there would control the gateway to Europe, Asia, and Africa.

Aristobulus I

Hyrcanus was succeeded by his son Aristobulus I. However, Hyrcanus had intended to leave the government of the state in the hands of his widow. Aristobulus resented this decision and put his mother in prison. Josephus wrote: "He intended to change the government into a kingdom, for so he resolved to do. First of all [Aristobulus] put a diadem on his head four hundred eighty and one years and three months after the people had been delivered from the Babylonish slavery."[14]

Aristobulus reigned only one year, but in that year he demonstrated how little, if anything, the Hasmonean dynasty had learned from the history of the past five centuries. Continuing the policies of his father, he conquered much of Iturea (Galilee) and, according to Josephus, forcibly compelled them "to be circumcised, and to live according to Jewish laws."[15]

Under Aristobulus I, Judaism rapidly embraced circumcised paganism. With incredible savagery he starved his mother to death in prison. He also imprisoned all of his brothers except one, Antigonus, for whom he seemed to have some affection. But Antigonus enraged Aristobulus by acting as high priest once during the feast of tabernacles while Aristobulus was sick, and Aristobulus murdered the only brother he loved. Aristobulus deeply regretted this act, although it is hard to believe that a man who could starve his own mother could suffer remorse.

Aristobulus's name was Judah in Hebrew, but Judea's leaders were becoming more Hellenized and he preferred the Greek name *Aristobulus*. To the people his name was a minor matter. After all, times do change. But when he resorted to murder, fratricide, and matricide, the people saw that their newly crowned king was acting just like the pagan kings of Egypt and Syria.

A rift was developing between the people and the throne; the Hasmonean dynasty was losing its legitimacy. Meanwhile the Pharisees were insisting that according to the Law and the Prophets, only someone belonging to the house and lineage of David could rightfully sit on Judea's throne.

When Aristobulus died of a horrible sickness one year after he was crowned, there was a national sigh of relief.

It is thought that the remorse he felt for killing Antigonus hastened his death.

Alexander Jannaeus

Aristobulus did not have any children. His widow, Salome Alexandra, immediately freed the king's three surviving brothers from prison. According to the law of levirate marriage (see Deuteronomy 25:5; Jewish law prescribed that a widow must marry her husband's brother who is also her own contemporary) Salome married Alexander Jannaeus, the oldest of the three brothers. Alexander became the new king and high priest.

The change of regime brought no change of policy. For fifteen years Alexander fought expansionist wars. Then in 89 B.C. while attacking the Arabs in the South, his armies were ambushed and almost surrounded. The ambushment was just the opportunity the Pharisees wanted. They thought that Alexander was about to be defeated and they planned a revolt. While Alexander was officiating as high priest on the next feast of tabernacles, at a prearranged signal the celebrants pelted him with the etrogim (citron) that each of them carried in his hand for the day's ritual. The Pharisees wanted to show Alexander that they felt the high priesthood had been desecrated.

Alexander was infuriated. He ordered his soldiers to charge into the throng and hundreds were killed. In desperation the Pharisees appealed to the king of Syria for help. Imagine the descendants of the Maccabees begging for help from the successors of Antiochus Epiphanes! The Syrians eagerly responded and the Pharisees joined their ranks.

Alexander was routed and he fled into the hills. However, the Pharisees soon realized that the Syrian king would attempt to resume authority over Judea, so hoping that Alexander had learned a lesson, thousands of them joined Alexander's armies. With the Pharisees' help, Alexander defeated the Syrians.

Restored to power, Alexander Jannaeus instituted a manhunt for the rebels. He made a horrible example of those he caught. F. F. Bruce wrote:

> Having thus re-established his control over his kingdom, he returned to his capital, taking the leaders of the die-hard rebels with him as captives. There he took a grim revenge. Eight hundred of them were crucified in full view of the royal palace, where the king and his concubines feasted their eyes on their torments; and while they were still alive on their crosses, their wives and children were brought out and butchered before their eyes.[16]

Effectively terrorized, eight thousand Pharisees fled to Arabia, Moab, and Gilead. Alexander "fell into a distemper by hard drinking" and died three years later.[17]

Salome Alexandra

On his deathbed in 76 B.C. Alexander bequeathed the throne to his wife, Salome Alexandra. Alexander evidently had learned a lesson concerning the Pharisees, for according to Josephus he instructed his wife to "put some of her authority in the hands of the Pharisees."[18] Salome did not need any great urging to carry out her husband's advice, for as Josephus stated succinctly, "She had indeed the name of the regent, but the Pharisees had the authority."[19] At the time of her accession, Salome was already sixty-four years old, but she proved to be one of the ablest and most noble rulers in Jewish history.

During her nine-year reign, the Pharisees became the dominant party in Judea. It is difficult to discern exactly what transpired between the Pharisees and the Sadducees during those years, for our only source of information is Josephus, and he was a Pharisee. There is no question that the Pharisees could not restrain their desire for revenge upon the Sadducees who had supported Alexander

Jannaeus. Their leader Diogenes was murdered and the tension between the Pharisees and Sadducees continued until the destruction of the temple in A.D. 70 when Sadduceeism was destroyed.

Under Salome Alexandra the Pharisees made one of the greatest contributions to Jewish life by decreeing that every Jewish boy must receive an education. (Her brother, Rabbi Simeon ben Shetach, was president of the Sanhedrin at the time.) Before the decree, education had been the responsibility of the family; after the decree, education became the responsibility of both the home and the community. Every synagogue became a school. The Jews living in Judea, and eventually those living all over the world, became a literate people, able to read and understand the Scriptures.

Salome had borne two sons to Alexander Jannaeus— Hyrcanus II and Aristobulus II. Josephus described them as follows: "Now, as to these two sons, Hyrcanus was indeed unable to manage public affairs, and delighted rather in a quiet life; but the younger, Aristobulus, was an active and a bold man."[20]

Aristobulus II versus Hyrcanus II

When Salome Alexandra became queen, she could not, being a woman, succeed her husband as high priest. She therefore appointed Hyrcanus, her elder son, to that office. She knew that he was not ambitious for power and would not challenge her queenly authority, so appointing him seemed to be the wise thing to do. At the same time she gave her younger, more ambitious son a military command.

Aristobulus was indeed an ambitious young man. With the support of the disgruntled Sadducees who longed for a return to power, he planned to overthrow his brother as quickly as possible. When Alexandra died in 67 B.C., Hyrcanus II automatically succeeded his mother to the throne and Aristobulus, who had already raised an army, immediately attacked his brother. Their armies clashed near Jericho, where many of the royal soldiers deserted to Aristobulus. Hyrcanus fled to Jerusalem and when his brother followed him, he abjectly surrendered. They made an agreement whereby Hyrcanus was permitted to retire to his estate unmolested and Aristobulus II became both king and high priest.

This arrangement undoubtedly pleased Hyrcanus. He was not competent to rule, and it would have been good for him and for Jewish history if he had been allowed to follow his natural desires and sink into obscurity. But Hyrcanus, as we will see, was not permitted to enjoy retirement.

Aristobulus had an enemy who at this point interfered in the history of Israel. His name was Antipater, the governor of Idumea (Edom), which had been conquered by John Hyrcanus I. (Antipater was the father of Herod the Great.) Antipater fomented a movement among the most powerful Jews. Josephus said he complained that "it was unjust to overlook the conduct of Aristobulus, who had gotten the government unrighteously, and ejected his brother from it, who was the elder, and ought to retain what belonged to him by prerogative of his birth."[21]

Antipater convinced Hyrcanus that Aristobulus planned to assassinate him. Antipater schemed with Aretas III, who was an Arabian (Nabatean) ruler, to support Hyrcanus in a revolt. At first Hyrcanus was entirely against taking action, but he ultimately yielded.

Hyrcanus and Antipater fled from Jerusalem to Petra. An agreement was made that Aretas would join with Hyrcanus's forces and attack Judea. As a reward Aretas would receive the twelve cities Alexander Jannaeus had taken from the Arabians. So Aretas and Hyrcanus invaded Judea. A battle was fought—Josephus does not give the location—and Aristobulus was beaten and compelled to retreat to Jerusalem. Many of Aristobulus's troops defected to Hyrcanus. Then the combined forces of Aretas and Hyrcanus attacked Jerusalem and besieged Aristobulus's forces stationed there.

THE RISE OF ROME

Pompey

While this revolt was taking place among the Jews, the face of western Asia was also changing, for the Roman general Pompey had been victorious in Syria. He could not afford to have fighting neighbors, so he settled the fight between Aristobulus and Hyrcanus. And Rome won!

Rome entered Judea in the person of General Scaurus, who had been sent to Syria by Pompey. By coming to Judea, Scaurus hoped to enhance his position and increase his power. He recognized the feuding of the two brothers as an opportunity for Rome to step in and for Scaurus to gain world recognition. The two brothers played right into his hands. As soon as Scaurus entered the country, both brothers sent personal ambassadors to seek his assistance. However, Aristobulus offered a gift of 300 talents of silver while Hyrancus made only a promise. Josephus wrote, "Aristobulus's 300 talents had more weight with him than the justice of the cause."[22] By accepting the gift from Aristobulus (worth approximately $1,500,000) and rejecting the promise of Hyrcanus, Scaurus showed to the Jewish nation that once again their throne and priesthood could be sold to the highest bidder.

Scaurus wasted no time showing his favoritism toward Aristobulus. He immediately threatened both Hyrcanus and Aretas by telling them that Pompey and the Romans would come unless they called off their siege of Jerusalem. Aretas fled to Philadelphia and Aristobulus chased after the rest of his enemies. He fought them and killed over six thousand. Among the dead was Phalion, Antipater's brother. With the death of his brother giving him even more reason to hate Aristobulus, Antipater told more seditious lies about Aristobulus to Hyrcanus. The lies and innuendoes added more fuel to the fire of hatred already separating the families of Aristobulus and Hyrcanus.

Aristobulus felt he had made a friend of Rome. Little

did he realize that the words of the prophet Daniel were to be fulfilled and that he would be one of the instruments used in their fulfillment. Heinrich Graetz wrote about the fateful days foretold by Daniel:

> More terrible than earthquakes or hurricanes was the harbinger of evil that appeared in Judaea. "The beast with iron teeth, brazen claws, and heart of stone that was to devour much and trample the rest under foot" which came to the Judaean nation to drink its blood, to eat its flesh, and to suck its marrow. The hour had struck when the Roman eagle with swift flight was to swoop down upon Israel's inheritance, circling widely, round the bleating nation, lacerating her with cruel wounds and finally leaving her a corpse.[23]

For two years Aristobulus was established as head of the state of Judea. He even had coins engraved with his image and name. But he was living in a fool's paradise, for while he played king of Judea, Hyrcanus convinced Scaurus that he should side with him. Hyrcanus also sought to gain favor with Pompey. Like Scaurus, Pompey saw the feud between the two brothers as an opportunity for himself and Rome to gain further control of the Middle East. Seizing the opportunity, he sided with Hyrcanus, since he was the weaker of the two brothers. Once Hyrcanus was restored to power, Pompey would give him a strong supporting prime minister who would force him to follow Rome's policies.

Aristobulus, seeing the handwriting on the wall, fortified himself in the citadel of Alexandria but was soon forced to succumb to the might and the greed of Rome. Leaving Alexandria, Aristobulus fled to Jerusalem and began to fortify the city walls from within. This was the beginning of the end for the city of Jerusalem and the country of Judea.

Aristobulus was determined to wage war on Pompey, but Pompey did not give him time to unite his forces.

Pompey started his march from his encampment in Jericho to Jerusalem. Realizing he had no time to prepare for war, Aristobulus left Jerusalem and met Pompey with expensive gifts and promises to surrender the city. However when Aristobulus returned to Jerusalem in the company of the Roman legate Gabinius, they found that the city gates had been locked and fortified from within by the Jewish patriots who did not want Jerusalem to fall into Gentile hands. At this point the followers of Hyrcanus, "lovers of peace," opened the gates of the city and let the forces of Pompey enter. The patriots then retreated to the temple mount and prepared to fight Pompey.

Realizing he was going to be in for a long siege, Pompey sent for the battering rams. Hoping to take advantage of the patriots' adherence to the Jewish laws, he planned to storm the fortress on the sabbath. Ordinarily these religious Jews would not pick up arms on the sabbath, but the interpreters of the law ruled that the patriots could resist an attack on the temple on the sabbath, although they could not defend the walls of the city on the sabbath. The Romans, learning of this distinction, stopped the attack on the temple fortress and began working on destroying the walls of the city. Finally on a sabbath in the month of Sivan (June) 63 B.C. the Romans were able to break through the walls and enter the city of Jerusalem. Josephus described how Pompey then entered the temple and the holy of holies:

> Of all the disasters of that period none wounded the nation to the heart so deeply as the exposure of the hither-to-concealed Holy Place to alien eyes. Indeed, together with his staff, Pompey entered the sanctuary which no one but the High Priest was permitted to enter and beheld its contents—the candelabrum, the lamps, the table, the vessels of lavation and censers, all of solid gold, an accumulation of spices, and a treasury of consecrated money totaling 2,000 talents—but he did not lay hands

either on these nor on any other sacred treasures and on the day after the capture he ordered a custodian to purify it and to resume the customary sacrifices.[24]

Once Pompey entered the holy of holies and found no idols and saw no images ridiculing Rome inscribed on the walls, he left the temple intact, since he did not want to be known as the "robber of the sanctuaries." Not having the temple destroyed was a blessing for Judaism. But there was a curse to follow, for when Pompey marched into the sanctuary, Judea lost its independence. From that time on, Jerusalem has remained under the domination of the Gentile nations, as the prophets foretold. The temple, which would ultimately be destroyed by the Romans in A.D. 70, continued to serve as a fortress—a place of seething revolution and reaction against Roman rule rather than a place to worship the living God.

Pompey leveled the walls of the city of Jerusalem and took Aristobulus prisoner as well as his sons Antigonus II and Alexander II. Pompey then reaffirmed Hyrcanus, who had assisted him in the defeat of Aristobulus, as high priest, but severely limited his duties and responsibilities. The high priest was to serve under the jurisdiction of the Roman proconsul at Damascus.

Pompey returned to Rome a hero, but his glory was short-lived. He was soon forced to flee by Julius Caesar, who claimed the Roman empire for himself. Pompey fled from Rome to Syria and joined forces with Antipater. In retaliation, according to Josephus, Julius Caesar released Aristobulus from prison and sent him to Syria with two legions of soldiers to wrest power from Antipater and Pompey. If Aristobulus succeeded, Syria and Judea could be subdued under Roman leadership. However before Aristobulus reached Syria, he was poisoned by friends of Antipater.[25]

When Aristobulus and his family were being transported to Rome as prisoners, his elder son Alexander escaped and returned to Judea, where he assembled an army of fifteen thousand horsemen and ten thousand foot soldiers. He marched on Jerusalem and forced Hyrcanus and Antipater to flee the city. Alexander attempted to set himself up as king and high priest—but it was not to happen!

All the time Aristobulus remained in prison, Alexander continued his insurrections against the Roman general Gabinius, who was then governor of Syria. In their final encounter Gabinius employed Antipater to persuade the soldiers of Alexander's army to desert to Hyrcanus, and many did. So Alexander was left with an army of thirty thousand men to fight against the combined armies of Hyrcanus and Gabinius. Alexander was soundly defeated and left without resources. Antipater, wanting Rome to give him the rulership of the Middle East, effected a reconciliation between Alexander and Hyrcanus by arranging a marriage between Alexander and Hyrcanus's daughter Alexandra. Such an alliance would give Alexander an opportunity to become the high priest—but, again, it was not to happen!

Shortly after Aristobulus was poisoned, Pompey and Antipater had Alexander (who was then in Antioch) executed by Pompey's father-in-law, Q. Caecilius Metellus Scipio, the proconsul of Syria. Antipater charged that Alexander had planned to join forces with his father and was therefore worthy of death.

With Alexander out of the way, Gabinius divided the country into five provinces and placed rulers who would be favorable to Rome in the five major cities (Jerusalem, Jericho, Gezer, Safed, and Chamas in Trans-Jordan). Gabinius also abolished the Sanhedrin, which had been meeting on the temple mount. According to the Talmud, "When the Sanhedrin was abolished songs were no longer heard at banquet halls" (Talmud: Sotah 48a).

With the Sanhedrin abolished, political power belonged solely to Rome. But Gabinius's regional plan was not to last for long. The Sanhedrin had been a central part of control and rule over Judea and its dissolution brought disunity to the country, so Gabinius allowed the Sanhedrin to reassemble, although it still could not exercise any political power. It could only rule in the areas of moral and religious issues.

Now known as the Great Sanhedrin, its president was Simon ben Shetach. He skillfully began replacing Sadducean members with men of Pharisaic background, thus changing the complexion of the Sanhedrin. With the Pharisees in control, he was able to restore Torah study and teaching and to implement strict interpretation of Jewish law and tradition. He gathered disciples in small study groups and began the first public education system in Israel. His desire was to teach the young so that when they matured, they would maintain a proper Jewish state.

Simon ben Shetach was succeeded by two of his disciples, Shemaya (Sameas) and Abtalion (Pollion). These men continued the strong tradition of teaching the Torah and Jewish law to small groups of disciples. All the while Shemaya and Abtalion were teaching Jewish tradition, Rome was establishing a tradition of its own: divide and conquer. During the entire period of the Great Sanhedrin (60–35 B.C.) the tiny country of Judea was feeling the tightening grip of Rome on its people and on its religion and traditions.

Julius Caesar

Rome's tightening grip on Judea was made possible by the involvement of Antipater and Hyrcanus II in the struggle between Julius Caesar and Pompey, who were locked in battle at Pharsalus in central Greece. Julius Caesar won the battle and then went on to Egypt with plans to conquer all of the Middle East. Antipater and Hyrcanus had been allies of Pompey, so now they feared for their lives. When they heard that Julius Caesar was losing the battle for the city of Alexandria in Egypt, Antipater made a shrewd move. He came to Julius Caesar's aid by supplying him with over three thousand Jewish soldiers.

Antipater was also able to convince the Egyptian Jews in Alexandria not to fight against the Romans. With the help of Antipater, Julius Caesar won the battle.

No sooner was the war over than Antipater appeared before Julius Caesar to claim his reward. Antipater had a specific request: he wanted the throne rights of Judea for himself. At the same time Antigonus II (the second son of Aristobulus II) came claiming his right to be installed as ruler of Judea because of his father's earlier assistance to Julius Caesar (when Aristobulus had set out to reclaim Syria and Judea). Caesar, himself a shrewd statesman, listened to the arguments of both men but finally ruled in favor of Antipater and Hyrcanus. Caesar reasoned that if he put Judea under the control of a non-Jew (Antipater was an Idumean), Rome would have better control over its territory and its peoples. As a reward for helping him in the battle against Pompey, Julius Caesar gave Antipater almost unlimited power and authority.

In 47 B.C. Julius Caesar officially appointed Hyrcanus to be the high priest and ethnarch *(nasi)*. He also gave Hyrcanus the right to pass the office to his descendants. By appointing Hyrcanus, a descendant of the Hasmonean line, to the high priesthood, Julius Caesar could cover his real motive—his intention was to give the real authority and power to a non-Jew. Hyrcanus was simply to be a figurehead, a puppet-priest for Antipater and, through Antipater, for Rome.

Caesar then allowed the Jews some freedom. They were permitted to rebuild the walls of Jerusalem and he returned to them the port city of Jaffa. Thus he disguised the iron fist of Rome in a velvet glove.

Herod the Great

Antipater had married Cypros, a beautiful woman from Arabia. They had four sons—Phasael, Herod, Joseph, and Pheroras—and a daughter Salome. Phasael, Herod, and Salome would each play a role in bringing Judea under the final control of Rome. Antipater appointed his eldest son Phasael to be the governor of Jerusalem. He appointed his second son Herod (who was then twenty years old) to be the governor of Galilee. Of the two sons, Herod was the stronger; like Esau and Jacob, the elder would eventually serve the younger. Graetz wrote of Herod:

> This prince was destined to become the evil genius of the Judaean nation. It was he who brought her as a bound captive to Rome; it was he who placed his feet triumphantly upon her neck. Like an ominous cloud weighed down with misfortune, he seems from the very first to have thrown a dark shadow upon the life of the nation, which, as it slowly but surely advanced, quenched all life in the gathering darkness and withered all growth, until nothing remained but a scene of desolation. True to his father's policy, Herod began by flattering Rome and by wounding the Judaean spirit.[26]

Galilee, over which Herod was made governor, was known for its patriotism. The people there refused to accept Roman rule. The province was growing in population, as it was one of the most fertile areas in the Middle East. The pressures of population increases and feelings of hostility against Rome made the area ripe for revolution. A Galilean by the name of Ezekius gathered about him a group of dissidents and led them in a revolt. Herod seized this opportunity to show both his strength and his allegiance to Rome. His actions at this time demonstrated a brutal nature that was to be characteristic of him throughout his reign. He arrested many of the young patriots along with their leader Ezekius and without any trial proceeded to have them executed.

According to Jewish law Herod should have been found guilty by the Sanhedrin and sentenced to death for mass murder. However, Rome had stripped the Jewish courts of all authority. They could only make recommendations to Rome. In outrage and despair the leaders and the people went to Hyrcanus II and demanded that he convene a special court that would have the prestige and authority to judge Herod. Graetz wrote:

> The bitter degradation which the people suffered at the hands of this Idumaean family inspired some of the most distinguished Judaeans to lay before the weak minded the true state of their own, and of their High Priest's new position. They explained to him that his dignity was but an empty name, that all real power lay with Antipater and his sons. They pointed to the execution of Ezekius and his followers as an act of gross contempt for the law. These bitter complaints would have had but little effect upon the weak Hyrcanus, had not the mothers of the slain torn his heart with their cries of anguish. Whenever he appeared in the Temple they threw themselves before him and entreated him not to let the death of their sons remain unavenged.[27]

Finally persuaded, Hyrcanus called together a special court over which he presided. Among some of the prominent sages who attended were Shammai and Avtalyon, outstanding teachers of the Torah, and members of the Sanhedrin. Herod was summoned to appear. Antipater warned him not to go into Jerusalem unarmed. So, knowing he was guilty, Herod surrounded himself with an armed escort and a letter from Sextus Caesar, governor of Syria, making the king of Judea responsible for Herod's life. Herod knew that by flexing the might of Rome he could frighten the Sanhedrin into releasing him.

He appeared before the Sanhedrin wearing his royal purple garments. His hair was styled in the grand Hellenistic manner and he was surrounded by his bodyguards. He should have been clothed in black in the manner of other individuals appearing before the court on criminal charges. Herod's appearance had its desired

effect. The entire court remained silent. Not one individual looked up. Finally, according to Josephus,
Shammai stood and said:

> O you that are assessors with me, and O thou that
> art our King, I neither have ever myself known such
> a case, nor do I suppose that any one of you can
> name its parallel, that one who is called to take his
> trial by us ever stood in such a manner before us;
> but everyone whosoever he be, that comes to be
> tried by this Sanhedrin, presents himself in a
> submissive manner, and like one that is in fear of
> himself, and that endeavors to move our com-
> passion, with his hair disheveled, and in a black and
> mourning garment; but this admirable man, Herod,
> who is accused of murder, and called to answer so
> heavy an accusation, stands here clothed in purple,
> and with the hair of his head finely trimmed, and
> with his armed men about him, that if we shall
> condemn him by our law, he may slay us, and by
> overbearing justice may himself escape death; yet
> do not I make this complaint against Herod himself:
> he is to be sure more concerned for himself than
> for the laws; but my complaint is against yourselves
> and your King, who give him a license so to do.
> However, take you notice, that God is great and that
> this very man, whom you are going to absolve and
> dismiss, for the sake of Hyrcanus, will one day
> punish both you and your king himself also.[28]

Once again in the so-called four hundred silent years
we see God speaking through a righteous man.
Shammai's words were prophetic. Indeed God does punish those who fail to live righteously.

The words of Shammai roused the Sanhedrin to action. They were about to vote a sentence of death upon
Herod when Hyrcanus stood up and commanded that
the court adjourn its meeting and postpone its verdict
until the next day. Herod left the court as arrogantly as

he had entered. He went directly to Damascus, where he met with Sextus Caesar, who then proclaimed him the military commander of Lebanon as well as Galilee. Fearing Herod, the court never reconvened and a verdict was never issued. Herod, desiring to avenge himself, was ready to ride with military troops from Lebanon into Jerusalem and slay all the members of the Sanhedrin, but his father calmed him down. However, Herod never forgot the incident and one day, as Shammai had predicted, Herod did avenge himself on the Sanhedrin.

On March 15, 44 B.C., after ruling the Roman empire for approximately three and one-half years, Julius Caesar was assassinated by Brutus and Cassius, and civil war broke out. Cassius took control of Syria, while Mark Antony, Octavius, and Lepidus took control of the rest of the empire. Caesar's former generals fought among themselves for power and control.

In order to end the civil war and come out victorious himself, Cassius ordered that taxes be levied on the inhabitants of Judah and Galilee (the territories he controlled) so that he could afford to raise an army to put down the rebellion. Those who would not or could not pay were sold into slavery. Antipater and his sons Phasael and Herod, who were appointed as tax collectors by Cassius, carried out their duties with great efficiency and cruelty. According to Josephus, "Herod was the first to satisfy Cassius with a quota of 100 talents from Galilee, and thereby became one of his best friends."[29]

Still not trusting God and so fearing man, Hyrcanus the high priest began to fear Antipater, the power his family had with Rome, and the control he had over Israel. Not alone in his fears, Hyrcanus found other Judeans who, like him, did not want to have an Idumean king ruling over them. Among them was Malichus, a zealot who conspired with Hyrcanus to poison Antipater.

Malichus was a tax collector hired by Antipater, along with his sons Phasael and Herod, to raise revenue for the Roman government. Malichus feigned friendship with Antipater and his sons and hid his deep hatred of them. On several occasions Malichus tried to have Antipater assassinated by foreign mercenaries. Trying a different tactic, Malichus deliberately refused to collect taxes, thinking Rome would reprimand Antipater or even execute him. But all of these strategies failed. Ironically Antipater, unaware of Malichus's plots, always came to his aid. Antipater's kindness seemed only to increase Malichus's hatred and his determination to do away with Antipater.

Patriotism was running high and the Jews wanted to rid themselves of this foreign king. Yet only a few years later they were asked by their foreign rulers if they wanted Jesus of Nazareth, a Jew, to be king and ruler over them, and the Jewish leaders responded, "We have no king but Caesar" (John 19:15).

At a great banquet Malichus bribed the royal cup-bearer to poison Antipater's drink. When Antipater rose to greet his friends and make a toast, he fell dead.

Ironically the assassination of Antipater by the Hasmonean supporters set off the chain of events that brought Herod to the Hasmonean throne and ultimately brought an end to the Hasmonean rule in Israel.

When Herod learned of his father's death, he could hardly wait to take revenge. When he found out that Malichus had instigated the poisoning of his father, he was ready to have him brutally killed. But Herod's brother Phasael persuaded him to wait until he could use his revenge on Malichus as a means of furthering his ambition. Phasael reasoned that if Herod openly killed Malichus, he would start a riot among the Judeans. Herod agreed and bided his time.

The appropriate moment came when the Roman general Cassius, Malichus, and Hyrcanus were in the area. Herod had learned that Malichus was intent on gaining the throne of Antipater for himself. Malichus had plotted that while Rome was involved with battles, he and his friends would assassinate Hyrcanus and take control of Judea. This plot gave Herod the opportunity and the motive to avenge his father's death and gain the favor of the Hasmonean supporters. Josephus told us what happened:

> Herod, perceiving this plan, invited both Hyrcanus and Malichus to dinner; he dispatched one of his servants to his home, as though to prepare the meal, but really to warn the tribunes to carry out the ambush. Remembering Cassius' orders, they made their way, sword in hand, to the shore facing the city, surrounded Malichus and stabbed him to death. Hyrcanus fainted from the shock; when he finally recovered consciousness he asked Herod who had murdered Malichus; one of the tribunes answered, "by Cassius' order." "Then," replied Hyrcanus, "Cassius has saved both me and my country by destroying the man who plotted against both." Whether he really thought so, or acquiesced from fear to an accomplished fact, remains unclear. At any rate, Herod thus avenged himself on Malichus.[30]

With the death of his father avenged, Herod immediately moved to make friends with Cassius. Herod's charms, his gifts, and his bribes as well as his military support worked and Cassius appointed him and Phasael to be the rulers in the land of Israel. However, a new threat to Herod arose. Mark Antony, Octavius, and Lepidus wanted the whole empire for themselves and they made war against Cassius and Brutus, defeating them at Philippi in 42 B.C.

To the victor go the spoils, so Mark Antony, Octavius (Augustus), and Marcus Aemilius Lepidus divided the territories among themselves. Mark Antony took over the territories of Asia, including Syria, Asia Minor, Judea, and Egypt. Octavius (Augustus) and Lepidus took over the West. Together the three leaders formed the second triumvirate approved by the Roman senate in 43 B.C. But their unity soon became division. Octavius became suspicious of Lepidus and took steps to curb his power and authority. Meanwhile Mark Antony and Cleopatra began a love affair that ignited a civil war and open conflict between the eastern and western divisions of the Roman empire.

The prophet Daniel, when interpreting Nebuchadnezzar's vision of a great statue, had spoken of a future kingdom that would be divided (Daniel 2:41). The division of the Roman empire into East and West became both its greatest strength and its greatest weakness. Once divided, the empire would never again be held together.

Herod now found himself in a very difficult situation. He had supported Cassius and Brutus, and now they were dead. How would Mark Antony, the new ruler, receive him? Herod also had a problem with the Jewish leaders from Judea who were hurrying to Antony to report his cruelties. They still wanted this foreign Idumean removed from power!

But Herod was not to be intimidated. In his sly and crafty way, bearing gifts and bribes, he appeared before Mark Antony. Herod recalled his earlier exploits for the Roman empire—the collecting of taxes for Cassius and the overthrowing of Aristobulus II, who had invaded Galilee in his attempt to capture the kingship of Judea. Herod convinced Antony that he could be of great service to him in repulsing the Parthians. He also led Antony to believe that if the Parthians were successful, they would give the throne of Judea to Antigonus, who would always be an implacable enemy of the Romans. Herod, on the other hand, would always be faithful to Rome!

Antony was completely deceived by the craft and subtlety of Herod. He saw in Herod an ally of Rome—someone he could count on to carry out his orders and help bring the Middle East under further control of Rome.

Strangely, Hyrcanus also appeared before Mark Antony and he too tried to persuade him to appoint Herod as governor. Antony was convinced and he appointed Phasael and Herod to be the governors of Judea with the title of tetrarch (governors or rulers of a fourth part of a country). Antony left Hyrcanus as the high priest, recognizing that the real power would rest with Herod.

What happened to other Judeans who appeared before Mark Antony? He imprisoned some and put others to death. Once again Rome was demonstrating its strength. Rome was in control!

Why Hasmonean Hyrcanus would support Idumean Herod as governor and ultimately king in Israel remains a mystery. People also wonder why Hyrcanus openly showed his support of the match when he announced that his granddaughter Mariamne was to be betrothed to Herod. What could have prompted such a marriage? Some scholars believe Herod wanted to marry the beautiful Mariamne for love. Others believe that he wanted to marry her for political and military reasons. But the real question is, Why would Hyrcanus support a marriage between a member of the Hasmonean family and the Idumean Herod?

Hyrcanus did not seem to be trusting God, but God uses the unbelief of men and their weaknesses to fulfill His purposes. During this time when He was preparing the world for the birth of His Messiah, He wanted to demonstrate the bankruptcy of a priesthood that could be bought and sold—the bankruptcy of a people who depended on manmade alliances rather than the covenants and promises of the living God. He also wanted to demonstrate that in the darkest hour of Israel's history a Messiah would come and bring light—not only to Israel but to all the nations of the world.

Perhaps Hyrcanus allowed Mariamne to be betrothed to Herod to protect his position when the Parthians defeated the Roman army near the border of Asia Minor. The Parthian general Barzaphernes had offered to the Hasmonean Antigonus II the throne of Judea if he would assist the Parthians. When Antigonus's earlier attempts to gain the support of the caesars had failed, he had joined an anti-Roman party in Judea and was now leading the opposition to Herod as well as the opposition to Hyrcanus. Antigonus felt that Hyrcanus was not the rightful heir to the high priesthood. Hyrcanus felt threatened by Antigonus, and perhaps Hyrcanus thought that by allowing his granddaughter to marry Herod, he could protect his own position and protect himself from the vengeance of Antigonus. Little did Hyrcanus realize the chain of events that would be unleashed by this marriage.

In 40 B.C. Barzaphernes and Antigonus forced the armies of Herod to take refuge behind the walls of Jerusalem during the festival of Sukkot (feast of tabernacles). At this time of year pilgrims would make their way up to Jerusalem to celebrate the feast, and many of those pilgrims joined the army of Antigonus in order to display their hatred for Herod. With increased numbers, Antigonus was able to force Herod's armies to surrender to the Parthians, and Jerusalem was captured by Barzaphernes. Herod managed to escape, but Hyrcanus was taken prisoner. Antigonus then ordered that both of Hyrcanus's ears be cut off, thus disqualifying him from ever again being a high priest. Herod's brother Phasael committed suicide. The Parthians took Hyrcanus back to Babylon. Herod, his family, and Mariamne all fled to Masada.

Antigonus was proclaimed king and high priest in 40 B.C. Impressed with his power and authority, he declared Judea to be an independent state. The coins he had minted read "Mattathias High Priest" on one side and "King Antigonus" on the other. There was general rejoicing, for the Judean state was at last free from foreign rulers, and a Hasmonean—a true descendant of David—was on the throne.

But the reign of Antigonus was to be short-lived; it lasted only until 37 B.C. Herod was already making plans to take revenge on Antigonus. Also, God had earlier decreed that the offices of king and priest were to be separate until the Messiah came. Only in Him would the two offices be combined (see Zechariah 6:10-15; Genesis 49:10). Whenever the kings of Israel violated this decree, they were punished: Saul, the first king of Israel, made this mistake and suffered for it. Successive generations of the Hasmonean leaders also sought to be king and high priest and were punished. Never learning from the mistakes of the past, Antigonus repeated the error and would now have to pay the price.

From Masada, Herod went to Egypt, and from Egypt he traveled to Rome. There the senate, at the recommendation of Mark Antony, proclaimed Herod king over the nation of Israel and declared Antigonus an enemy of Rome, thus sealing his fate. But Herod was, in fact, a king without a kingdom. Before he could rule, he had to regain his country from the control of Antigonus.

Herod departed from Rome a hero. He had the full support of the Roman senate and the might of Rome backing him. He headed for Syria, where the Roman proconsul supplied him with a large army. Herod and his army marched first through Galilee. The Galileans, knowing his cruelty and heavy taxations, fought him. Antigonus sent his armies to assist the local people, but nothing could stop the revenge and ambition of Herod.

Rome had proclaimed him king of the Jews, but he was not a Jewish king. In an attempt to correct this flaw, Herod married Mariamne in 37 B.C. Since she was a Hasmonean, by marrying her he became a kinsman of the kingly line. Herod would do anything to fulfill his ambition.

Having been declared king, having gained the rights of king through marriage, and having conquered Galilee, Herod led his Roman army to the gates of Jerusalem.

Herod was hated by the Judeans, but because of his personal charisma and clever ways he was able to make friends in high places and win over many of the ordinary people. Antigonus, on the other hand, had no charm. Graetz wrote of him:

> Even amongst his own people Antigonus did not know the secret of winning men of influence to his cause so that they would stand or fall with him. The very leaders of the Sanhedrin, Shammai and Avtalyon, adverse to Herod on account of his

overwhelming audacity, were not partisans of Antigonus. It is somewhat difficult to understand entirely the reasons for this aversion to this Hasmonaean king. Had Antigonus professed allegiance to the Sadducean principles, or was there a personal jealousy between the representatives of the royal power and the teachers of the law? We're led to believe from one circumstance, insignificant in itself, that the dislike originated from the latter cause. It happened once, on the Day of Atonement, that the entire congregation, according to custom, had followed the High Priest, Antigonus, at the close of the divine service, from the Temple to his own residence. On the way they met the two Sanhedrists, Shammai and Avtalyon; they quitted their priest-king to form an escort for their beloved teachers of the law. Antigonus, vexed at this apparent insult, expressed his displeasure to the Sanhedrists by an ironical obeisance, which they returned in the same offensive way. This unfortunate variance with the most influential men, coupled with Antigonus' lack of Generalship and statecraft, brought misfortune upon himself, his house, and the nation.[31]

The victories of Herod and the unpopularity of Antigonus weakened the leadership of Antigonus and the loyalty of his men. After five months of siege and intense fighting, Jerusalem fell to the forces of Herod. The final battle for the city took place on a sabbath evening when the Judean soldiers were least expecting an attack. The Romans breached the wall, ran into the city, and slaughtered any and all they came across. They killed without discrimination as to age or sex. They even murdered priests beside their sacrifices. Tradition holds that Jerusalem fell on the anniversary of the very day on which, twenty-seven years earlier, the temple had been taken by General Pompey. Herod, the king without a kingdom, now had one. It was a rebellious kingdom of leaders and people who would not accept him, but a kingdom he would subdue by force. Ultimately many of the leaders and many of the people would transfer their allegiance to him and to Rome.

Ironically within a few years another King came who was not received. He was declared to be King by God, but He too was rejected by the leaders of the people. However He did not subdue His kingdom by force. His kingdom was subdued through love.

Antigonus was taken alive and sent in chains to Syria. At the request of Herod, Mark Antony had Antigonus beheaded. All those who had been loyal to Antigonus were then put to death by Herod. He also took revenge on the members of the Sanhedrin who twelve years earlier had brought him to trial for the murder of Ezekius. Every one of them was killed, except Avtalyon and Shammai, the two who had been hostile to Antigonus. Interestingly, Shammai had spoken out against Herod in his trial. Then to enrich his royal treasury, Herod seized the properties of all those he had executed.

Only four members of the Hasmonean family remained alive when Herod captured Jerusalem: Hyrcanus II; his daughter Alexandria; her daughter, Queen Mariamne; and Aristobulus III, the son of Alexandria and Alexander II.

Herod realized that in order to consolidate his power he would have to watch carefully at least two of the four surviving members of the Hasmonean family: his sixteen-year-old brother-in-law, Aristobulus III; and the aged Hyrcanus. Herod was really more fearful of Aristobulus than he was of Hyrcanus.

Hyrcanus had been living in Babylon since the Parthian capture of Jerusalem and had become very popular among the Babylonian-Judean community. Herod sensed that Hyrcanus might become too popular and cause him difficulty with the Jews of the diaspora, so he extended an invitation to Hyrcanus to return to Jerusalem. The Babylonian Jews tried to warn him about Herod's plans, but to no avail. The aged Hasmonean was longing to return and when he arrived, Herod bestowed every honor on him. It was Herod's desire that Hyrcanus remain in Jerusalem so he could keep an eye on him and use him to fulfill his political ambitions.

Since Hyrcanus could not serve as high priest because of his mutilation, Herod chose Ananel (Hananeel) of Babylon to be the high priest in Jerusalem. Herod could have chosen Aristobulus III, but he wanted to bypass the Hasmonean line. Ananel was from the Zadokite family and it was believed that he was from the line of Aaron, though not through the high-priestly line.

Herod used the appointment of Ananel to support the rumor that he himself came from an old Judean family that had returned from Babylon. He wanted to obliterate the fact that his Idumean ancestors had been forced to convert to Judaism. The natives of Jerusalem and Judea knew better, but the strangers and newcomers believed these rumors. Herod was seeking to establish his Jewishness and his right to the throne of David.

As sly and shrewd as Herod was in bypassing Aristobulus III for the priesthood, he underestimated the anger of Alexandria, the mother of Aristobulus and mother-in-law of Herod. She put pressure on Herod to appoint Aristobulus and when Herod refused, she appealed directly to her friend, Cleopatra of Egypt, the wife of Mark Antony. Alexandria asked Cleopatra, who she knew hated Herod, to ask her husband to convince Herod that Aristobulus should be made high priest.

To please Cleopatra, Mark Antony told Herod that he would have to place Aristobulus in the office of high priest and remove Ananel. Technically such a removal was against Judaic law, since the high priest was appointed for life. However, Herod the politician did not want to displease Mark Antony, so he disregarded the law, removed Ananel, and installed seventeen-year-old Aristobulus as the high priest.

Alexandria still was not satisfied. She was determined to see that her son was king as well as high priest. Instead of the cruel Idumean Herod, she wanted Aristobulus to wear the crown his Hasmonean ancestors had worn.

Encouraged by Alexandria, Aristobulus grew in popularity. When he officiated at the feast of tabernacles, his aristocratic bearing and handsome appearance deeply impressed the people. Everyone rejoiced to see him and praised him. On the other hand, everyone showed contempt and hatred for Herod. His bodyguards had to accompany him wherever he went. He knew he was king over a kingdom where only a few showed him love and respect; the majority wanted him replaced. Herod knew Aristobulus would be the people's choice.

Fearing a popular revolt, Herod devised a plot to get rid of young Aristobulus. He invited Alexandria and Aristobulus to join him and other family members in Jericho. While they were there, Herod demonstrated affection for Aristobulus. Little did Aristobulus know that accepting "friendship" from Herod would cost him his life. One hot day Herod invited Aristobulus to his pool. Herod had bribed some of his servants and soldiers to mock-play with Aristobulus in the pool and at an appropriate time hold his head under the water until he drowned. His death was to appear to be an accident. They quickly followed Herod's instructions.

According to Josephus, Herod feigned grief. He made gala funeral arrangements and buried Aristobulus in an expensive tomb. Herod played his role very well. Then he reappointed Ananel and proceeded with his plans to establish himself as king.

But the killing of Aristobulus brought nothing but grief to Herod. The familiar adage "Be sure your sins will find you out" was very applicable to Herod. Alexandria knew that her son's death was no accident; she knew that Herod had deliberately had him killed. She also realized that her ambition for the throne could never be fulfilled, so she began to plot her revenge on Herod. Once again she contacted her friend Cleopatra. This time Alexandria convinced both Mark Antony and Cleopatra of Herod's guilt.

Mark Antony promptly summoned Herod to Laodicea to answer the charges of Alexandria. Herod, being a sly old fox, knew Mark Antony could have him killed, so when he went to Laodicea, he put Mariamne under house arrest. She was left under the supervision of Joseph, Herod's brother, who had strict instructions to kill Mariamne immediately if Herod was killed.

Having taken steps to ensure that no Hasmonean could take control of his throne, Herod prepared to save his life and his kingdom. He met Mark Antony with flattering words and expensive gifts and bribes, but Mark Antony drew a hard bargain. In exchange for his life, Herod had to give Mark Antony the rich and fertile district of Jericho. Antony wanted Jericho as a gift for Cleopatra.

His life preserved, and still having a kingdom, Herod happily returned to Jerusalem. But he was met with alarming news from Salome, the wife of Joseph. She told Herod that in his absence Mariamne and Joseph had engaged in an affair. In a fit of rage Herod ordered the immediate execution of his own brother Joseph. Only Herod's great love for Mariamne kept him from having her killed as well. He believed Alexandria was behind the story of Mariamne's adulterous behavior and therefore had Alexandria placed in chains and under house arrest.

The seeds of distrust that had been planted between Herod and Mariamne continued to grow. Herod became suspicious of everyone. He saw plots and evil schemes behind every conversation and every friendship. He was in subjugation to his paranoia and although it ultimately led to his sickness and death, it was the stage on which God's drama of redemption was played out. The characters in the drama included a sinful illegitimate king who ruled over a spiritually bankrupt priesthood and a people who were being held captive by a foreign nation. Onto that stage of Herod's paranoia, God sent His Messiah, Yeshua of Nazareth. Ironically, He too was proclaimed to be illegitimate by the Jewish rulers. Within the redemptive program of God, the Messiah too was perceived by the Herods as a threat to their throne rights and He too became a victim of their hatred.

Meanwhile Cleopatra decided she wanted to get rid

of Herod and take over Judea herself. She devised a plan in which Herod became involved in a war with the Nabatean king Malchus. But her plan backfired and instead of losing the war, Herod was victorious.

While Cleopatra plotted, the so-called Judean Sibyl began to prophecy the coming destruction of the Greek-Roman state and foretell the coming of a Messiah who would destroy the pagan Belial ruling over Judea.[32]

The news that Octavius Caesar had defeated Mark Antony in the battle of Actium on September 2, 31 B.C., brought a new challenge to Herod. He now had to convince Octavius that he was his friend and the legitimate ruler of Judea. But for Herod, who had become a master of deceit, this was not a difficult task. As soon as he heard of Mark Antony's defeat, he forbade all his armies to go through Syria in an attempt to help Mark Antony. Herod used this ploy to persuade Octavius that he had helped him win his victory over Mark Antony.

But Herod still was not going to take any chances about his right to the throne of David. Before leaving for Rhodes to meet with Octavius, Herod devised a scheme to do away with Hyrcanus, the only remaining Hasmonean. Herod accused Hyrcanus of plotting with the Nabateans to have him overthrown. Having firmly established this lie, Herod had Hyrcanus quickly executed. And Herod put his wife Mariamne and her mother Alexandria under the care of his closest friends, Joseph and Soemus. Their instructions were to put the women to death if Herod died or was killed.

Having in his own mind secured his kingdom for his sons, Herod left for Rhodes, where he convinced Octavius of his loyalty. In return Octavius gave back all of Jericho to Herod and added Gadara, Hippos, Samaria, Gaza, Anthedon, Joppa, and Strato's Tower (which later became Caesarea) to his kingdom. Octavius also confirmed Herod's right to the throne.

Herod was finally gaining his long-sought-after kingdom, but his personal life was about to fall apart; his sins were catching up with him. While he was in Rhodes,

Mariamne learned of Herod's intent to have her killed if he should die. She was livid with anger and her anger was used against her by Herod's Idumean relatives. They began to spread the rumor that Mariamne was trying to poison Herod. The rumors became too much for Herod, so in spite of his great love for her, he had Mariamne executed in the year 29 B.C.

The execution of Mariamne only aggravated Herod's problems and he went into a deep depression. Some historians say he went mad or was on the verge of insanity. He vented his wrath on everyone around him. He executed those who had executed Mariamne and when he heard that Alexandria was plotting to take over his kingdom, he had her executed. And when his sister Salome told Herod that her husband Costobarus, who was the governor of Idumea, was planning a revolt, Herod had Costobarus and all of his followers executed. This action pleased Salome, as she wanted her husband killed.

Although Herod had done away with the last male Hasmonean contender for the throne, the Talmud relates a legend concerning a young girl who was a surviving member of the Hasmonean family (Talmud: Baba Bathra 3b). Some scholars believe the legend refers to Mariamne, the daughter of Alexander, a son of Aristobulus II. The Talmud states that Herod wanted to marry her in order to assure his dynasty; but not wanting to marry Herod, the girl committed suicide by throwing herself off a rooftop. From that time on the rabbis ruled that anyone who claimed Hasmonean descent should be considered a descendant of a non-Jewish slave. They reasoned that Herod, because of his Idumean descent, was really only a slave to the Hasmonean family. Thus any of his descendants could only be slaves and could never be legitimate kings.

In time Herod recovered from his illness. Feeling more secure, he began great building projects to promote himself as the legitimate king and ruler of Judea. Rome accepted him as king, his fellow Idumeans accepted him as king, and the Gentiles within the empire accepted him as king, but most of the Jewish people did not accept him as a legitimate king. They were looking for a coming Messiah, a ruler who would throw off the yoke of Rome.

In 24 B.C. Herod had six thousand Torah scholars in Jerusalem killed because they would not take an oath of loyalty to him. In reality Herod was afraid of these Jewish teachers and rabbis, as he thought that they were plotting to overthrow him. According to the Talmud, after Herod executed the six thousand rabbis, he disguised himself and went out among the people to find out exactly what the rabbis had been saying. He could not find one rabbi who would curse him or speak ill of him. He was so impressed with the circumspection of the rabbis that he said:

> I am Herod. Had I known that the rabbis were so circumspect, I should not have killed them. Now tell me what amends I can make....He [Rabbi Baba b. Buta] replied: As you have extinguished the light of the world, [for so the Rabbis are called] as it is written, *For the commandment is a light and the Torah is a lamp*, go now and attend to the light of the world [which is the Temple, of which] it is written, *And all nations become enlightened by it*. Some report that Baba b. Buta answered him thus: As you have blinded the eye of the world, [for so the Rabbis are called] as it is written, *If it be done unwittingly by the eyes of the congregation*, go now and attend to the eye of the world, [which is the Temple]*, as it is written, *I will profane my sanctuary, the pride of your power, the delight of your eyes.* (Talmud: Baba Bathra 4a).

This interesting passage in the Talmud is said to contain the reason Herod was allowed to rebuild the temple. Why else would the Jewish leaders be willing? Herod was Idumean, not Jewish. He was not of Hasmonean descent, for his family had converted to Judaism years earlier. He was a man who had obtained the kingship of Judea through trickery, fraud, and murder. He was a puppet of

Rome, not the deliverer or the redemptive messiah whom the Jewish leaders expected or desired. Perhaps they thought that if the temple were rebuilt, the Messiah would come and the Messianic age would begin. This has certainly been the hope of Judaism through the years. It is the hope of orthodox Jews today.

If the rabbis in Herod's day were indeed thinking that if the temple were rebuilt, the Messiah would come, the visits of Yeshua (Jesus) to Herod's temple have even more significance. During one of His many visits to the temple He declared Himself to be the Messiah and equal with God (John 10:22-39). In Herod's temple He chased out the money-changers, turned over their tables, and castigated them for making the temple a place of merchandise (John 2:13-17). In Herod's temple He used the temple as a symbol of Himself (2:18-22).

The desire of the rabbis for the temple to be rebuilt so that the Messiah would come was fulfilled. Herod was rebuilding the temple when Yeshua was born in fulfillment of prophecy. It is ironic that the very Messiah the nation of Israel longed for came unto His own, but they failed to recognize Him. Instead they accepted as king the one who rebuilt the temple. They accepted an impostor instead of the One who was the Temple Himself, God manifest in the flesh, the eternal King of Israel and the world.

Construction of Herod's temple began in 20 B.C. and it was completed in A.D. 63. At the time Yeshua was teaching in the temple, forty-six years of building had already elapsed (John 2:20). After the temple was finished, it only stood for seven short years, for it was destroyed by Titus in A.D. 70. Herod did not live to see the temple completed, but it was his crowning achievement. The Talmud says:

> He who has not seen the Temple of Herod has never seen a beautiful building. Of what did he build it? Rabbah said: Of yellow and white marble. Some say, of blue, yellow and white marble. Alternate rows [of the stones] projected, so as to leave a place for

cement. He originally intended to cover it with gold, but the Rabbis advised him not to, since it was more beautiful as it was, looking like the waves of the sea (Talmud: Baba Bathra 4a).

As beautiful as the temple was, and as much as it contributed to the pride and growing nationalism of the Jewish people, it did not help make Herod and his family any more acceptable to the people of Israel. In fact the higher taxes levied on Herod's subjects to finance his expansive building projects only served to increase the people's hatred of him. Violence, civil unrest, and political and family intrigue continued to plague Herod.

According to Josephus, Herod had a total of ten wives, each of whom wanted her son to be king after Herod's death.[33] Herod's favorite sons were Alexander and Aristobulus, the children of Mariamne. They were to be his heirs. However, other family members told Herod that these two sons were plotting to kill him because he had killed their mother. Enraged, Herod called in his eldest son Antipater to control Alexander and Aristobulus, and named Antipater his sole heir.

Antipater, wanting to make sure that Herod would not change his mind, sent Herod slanderous and inflammatory letters about Alexander and Aristobulus. These letters made Herod so angry that he requested that these sons be tried and executed before Caesar Augustus. However, the trial resulted in an unexpected family reconciliation rather than the planned execution and Herod created another will in which he named all three sons as heirs.[34]

But the sons were too much like their father. They were not content to share the empire; each wanted it all for himself. Antipater once again began a series of plots, seeking to discredit other family members or have them murdered in order to make himself the sole heir. His tactics worked. Herod readily believed his lies and once again made him sole heir and successor to his throne.

Knowing Herod to be fickle, and anxious to ensure

his inheritance, Antipater devised a plot with Pheroras to kill Herod, even though he was in poor health. Pheroras was Herod's brother who was the tetrarch of Perea. The plot was simple: they would arrange to have Herod poisoned and place the blame on other family members. But the plot backfired. Herod's sister Salome revealed to Herod that Pheroras and Antipater were planning to have him murdered, and instead of Herod being poisoned, Pheroras himself was poisoned.

When Herod investigated the death of Pheroras, he was told by the slaves that Pheroras was poisoned with the very poison that Antipater had intended to use on him. Without revealing his wrath Herod sent for Antipater. As soon as he arrived, Herod had him arrested and began to arrange for his trial and execution. In the meantime Herod once again drafted a new will in which he left everything to his youngest son Antipas, the child of his Samaritan wife Malthace.[35]

Herod could find no peace. His illnesses increased and his mental phobias deepened as he became bent on revenge. He knew he was dying, yet he refused to repent; he refused to recognize God. Josephus believed that Herod's illness was a direct result of his sin, that his pain increased as a result of God's increasing judgment as he continued to sin without repentance. Josephus wrote: "But now Herod's distemper greatly increased upon him after a severe manner, and this by God's judgment upon him for his sins: for a fire glowed in him slowly, which did not so much appear outwardly, as it augmented his pains inwardly."[36] (The historian went on to describe in vivid detail the effect these illnesses had upon Herod.)

In his pain and sickness Herod ordered the execution of his son Antipater and once again changed his will. This was the final change before his death. In this last will he made Archelaus, the older son of Malthace, king; Archelaus's brother Antipas, tetrarch of Galilee and Perea; and their half brother Philip, tetrarch of Gaulanitis, Trachonitis, Batanea, and Paneas.[37]

Just before his death Herod took his final vengeance on the Jews. The story of his revenge involves two rabbis: Judas, son of Saripheus, and Matthias, son of Margalothus. Knowing that Herod was near death or had died, these two famous scholars of the Torah incited the people to riot. The rioters tore down the Roman eagle that Herod had erected over the great gate of the temple. When Herod found out what had happened, he ordered that the rabbis be bound in chains and brought to him. He then called together all the elders and rulers of the Jews. Too ill to stand, Herod lay on his couch as he rehearsed all that he had done to help the Jews. Jospehus wrote:

> He lay upon a couch, and enumerated the many labors he had long endured on their account, and his building of the temple, and what a vast charge that was to him; while the asamoneans *[sic]*, during the 125 years of their government, had not been able to perform any so great a work for the honor of God as that was: that he had also adorned it with very valuable donations; on which account he hoped that he had left himself a memorial, and procured himself a reputation after his death. He then cried out, that these men had not abstained from affronting him, even in his lifetime, but that, in the very daytime, and in sight of the multitude, they had abused him to that degree, as to fall upon what he had dedicated, and in that way of abuse, had pulled it down to the ground.[38]

In retaliation Herod had both rabbis killed; he commanded that Matthias be burned alive. Herod also ordered that all the Jewish rabbis, scholars, and leading men come to see him on his deathbed. Disobedience to this direct order of the king meant death. When they arrived, Herod went into a wild rage, accusing them of plots against him and of not appreciating all he had done for them. He ordered that they all be shut up in the great hippodrome. He sent for his sister Salome and her husband Alexas and told them:

> I shall die in a little time, so great are my pains; which death ought to be cheerfully borne, and to be welcomed by all men; but what principally troubles me is this, that I shall die without being lamented, and without such mourning as men usually expect at a king's death.[39]

Herod told Salome and Alexas to order the soldiers surrounding the hippodrome to slaughter everyone imprisoned there as soon as he was dead, before anyone else was told of his death. Herod's reasoning was recorded by Josephus:

> This slaughter of them all will cause that he [Herod] shall not miss to rejoice on a double account; that as he is dying, they will make him secure that his will shall be executed in what he charges them to do; and that he shall have honor of a memorable mourning at his funeral....So he deplored his condition, with tears in his eyes, and obtested them by the kindness due from them, as of his kindred, and by the faith they owed to God, and begged of them that they would not hinder him of this honorable mourning at his funeral. So they promised him not to transgress his commands.[40]

Herod, the would-be king of the Jews, died in his favorite city, Jericho, in the spring of 4 B.C., five days after he had ordered his son Antipater's execution. His last wishes were never carried out. God overruled and Salome and Alexas released all of the Jews being held in the hippodrome. Herod went to his grave with the fresh blood of his son on his hands and not knowing that his Satanic plot to destroy the Jews would fail. With the usual pomp and circumstance, but without the great mourning of the Jewish people that Herod had so carefully planned, Herod's son Archelaus was pro-claimed the new king.

THE END OF SPIRITUAL EXILE

Only a few years earlier, while Herod had been plot-ting to secure a place for one of his sons as his successor, magi from the East came inquiring about One who had been born King of the Jews (Matthew 2:1-12). The Scrip-tures tell us that Herod inquired diligently of these wise men; he wanted to know exactly where this King was born and at what time He was born. When the wise men failed to return to Herod to report their findings, he ordered that all male Jewish children two years of age and under be executed (2:16-18).

Herod knew he was a usurper of the throne. He knew from the rabbis that a real King of the Jews was to come. He knew from the Sibylline oracles that a Messiah, a Re-deemer, was to come who would throw off the yoke of Rome and rule from Jerusalem. At all costs, Herod was determined to hang on to his throne—a throne he had protected from the Hasmoneans by killing them one by one, a throne he had sought to protect through a mass slaughter of Jewish children. Herod's greed and diaboli-cal plots brought grief and pain to himself and many others and ultimately he failed.

But God's victorious plan began to unfold in the little village of Bethlehem. In fulfillment of His promises the rightful heir to the throne of David—the Messiah, the Son of God—was born. He was the living Temple, the Lion of Judah, the Root of David, the Lamb of God who would take away the sin of the world. He was called *Yeshua* ("Salvation") because He would save His people from their sins.

As Hebrews 1:1 reminds us, God had faithfully spo-ken to the Jewish people through the prophets at many times and in various ways. Hebrews 1:2 goes on to say, "But in these last days he has spoken to us by his Son." In the fullness of time Yeshua came unto His own to be their King-Priest.

But the nation was not ready to listen to Him. He presented Himself as King, but was mocked and rejected. The leaders cried out, "We have no king but Caesar" (John 19:15). The King of the Jews—the legitimate King of the Jews—was handed over to the Romans and was crucified.

The nation of Israel did not realize that through this one act of rejection their long years of exile would be extended. Nor did they realize that in their rejection of Yeshua as King and in His subsequent death at the hands of the Romans, His office of priest was fulfilled. His death and resurrection provided salvation, forgiveness of sin, and the end of spiritual exile to all who trust in Him. Spiritual exile ends for both Jew and Gentile when they accept Yeshua as their personal Messiah and Savior. But national exile for the Jewish people will only end when Yeshua comes again.

So history continues to unfold. All creation awaits that wonderful day of redemption when the Messiah will return to Israel. In that day He will gather the exiles and the outcasts of the nations and of Israel—all who have placed their faith and trust in Him—and will usher them into His glorious kingdom!

Notes

Introduction

1. In using the name *Yahweh,* LaSor transliterated the Hebrew *YHWH.* The original Hebrew Scriptures did not have any vowel signs and nobody really knows the correct pronunciation. The rabbis call it "The Ineffable Name" and never pronounce it.
2. William Sanford LaSor, "1 and 2 Kings" in *The New Bible Commentary: Revised,* ed. D. Guthrie et al. (Grand Rapids: Eerdmans, 1970) 321.
3. Will Durant, *The Story of Civilization* (New York: Simon and Schuster, 1935) 1:235.
4. Herodotus, 1.199.

Chapter 1

1. Frederick A. Tatford, *The Climax of the Ages* (Grand Rapids: Zondervan, 1964) 92-93.
2. Alexander Whyte, *Bible Characters from the Old and New Testaments* (Grand Rapids: Kregel, n.d.) 1:400-401.
3. "Redemption" in *Encyclopedia of the Jewish Religion,* ed. Zwi Werblowsky and Geoffrey Wigoder (New York: Adama, 1986) 327.
4. *The New Scofield Bible* (London: Oxford University Press, 1967) 832.
5. C.E. and B.C.E. are often used by historians, especially Jewish scholars, to denote the calendar change before and after the birth of Jesus. Used interchangeably, B.C. may mean "before Christ" and B.C.E., "before the common era." C.E.

may mean "the common era" or "the Christian era." C.E. is used by most Jewish writers rather than A.D., which comes from the Latin *anno Domini,* meaning "in the year of our Lord."

6. *Encyclopedia Judaica* (Jerusalem: Keter, 1972) 3:935.
7. Charles R. Eerdman, *The Book of Ezekiel: An Exposition* (Westwood, NJ: Revell, 1956) 11.
8. Roland K. Harrison, *Introduction to the Old Testament* (Grand Rapids: Eerdmans, 1969) 853.
9. Arno C. Gaebelein, *The Prophet Daniel* (New York: Our Hope, 1911) 9-10.

Chapter 2

1. Solomon Grayzel, *A History of the Jews* (Philadelphia: Jewish Publication Society, 1967) 16-17.
2. Charles F. Pfeiffer, *Between the Testaments* (Grand Rapids: Baker, 1959) 12.

Chapter 3

1. Charles L. Feinberg, *Daniel: The Kingdom of the Lord* (Winona Lake, IN: B.M.H. Books, 1984) 70.
2. Max I. Dimont, *Jews, God and History,* rev. ed. (New York: Penguin Books, Mentor Printing, 1994) 69-70.
3. F. F. Bruce, *Israel and the Nations* (Grand Rapids: Eerdmans, 1963) 100. Quotations from this book are used by permission of Paternoster Press.
4. Pfeiffer, *Between the Testaments,* 18-19.
5. H. L. Ellison, *From Babylon to Bethlehem* (Philadelphia: Westminster, 1979) 8. Quotations from this book are used by permission of Paternoster Press.
6. Flavius Josephus, *Antiquities of the Jews* 11.1.2.
7. Ellison, *From Babylon to Bethlehem,* 41.
8. Ibid., 42-43.
9. Bruce, *Israel and the Nations,* 107.
10. Grayzel, *History of the Jews,* 30.
11. Ellison, *From Babylon to Bethlehem,* 45.
12. *Encyclopedia Judaica* 12:1439.
13. Arno C. Gaebelein, *Gaebelein's Concise Commentary on the Whole Bible* (Neptune, NJ: Loizeaux, 1985) 403.

14. Bruce, *Israel and the Nations*, 117.
15. "Synagogue" in *Encyclopedia of the Jewish Religion*, 369.

Chapter 4

1. Will Durant, *The Life of Greece* (New York: Simon and Schuster, 1939) 238.
2. Dimont, *Jews, God and History*, 82-83.
3. Durant, *The Life of Greece*, 538.
4. Ellison, *From Babylon to Bethlehem*, 70.
5. Durant, *The Life of Greece*, 551.
6. Bruce, *Israel and the Nations*, 123.
7. Ibid., 124-125.
8. The Letter to Aristeas mentioned in Talmud: Megilla 9a is a part of the Old Testament pseudepigraphical literature. It dates between 250 B.C. and A.D. 100. Many scholars believe The Letter to Aristeas was written by a Jew living in Alexandria, Egypt. For a full translation see *The Old Testament Pseudepigrapha*, ed. James H. Charlesworth (Garden City, NY: Doubleday, 1985) 2:7-34.
9. Pfeiffer, *Between the Testaments*, 85.
10. Dimont, *Jews, God and History*, 86.
11. Harold A. Sevener, *God's Man in Babylon—The Visions and Prophecies of Daniel* (Charlotte, NC: Chosen People Ministries, 1994) 101.
12. Pfeiffer, *Between the Testaments*, 79-80.
13. Bruce, *Israel and the Nations*, 131.
14. Heinrich Graetz, *History of the Jews* (Philadelphia: Jewish Publication Society, 1967) 1:451-454.
15. Geoffrey W. Bromiley, ed., *The International Standard Bible Encyclopedia*, 4 vols. (Grand Rapids: Eerdmans, 1986) 1:16.
16. Graetz, *History of the Jews* 1:466.

Chapter 5

1. Josephus, *Antiquities of the Jews* 12.6.1.
2. *Encyclopedia Judaica* 7:1455.
3. Josephus, *Antiquities of the Jews* 12.9.4.
4. Trypho was a general who had served under Alexander Balas, an impostor who claimed to be the son of Antiochus Epiphanes and the only legitimate heir to his empire.

When Alexander died, Trypho attempted to gain control of the Seleucid empire. Seeking to depose the reigning monarch (Demetrius II Nicator), Trypho declared Antiochus VI Dionysus, the young son of Alexander Balas, to be the rightful heir to the throne (see Apocrypha, 1 Maccabees 11:39 ff.). Trypho's plan was to defeat Demetrius, set Antiochus up as a puppet king, and retain the power of the monarchy for himself. In his struggle with Demetrius, Trypho enlisted the help of Jonathan and his brother Simon by offering them key appointments in his administration. Jonathan, a military and political strategist, decisively defeated the armies of Demetrius at Hazor in 144 B.C. and Hamath in 143 B.C. However, the military victories of Jonathan and the increasing political and economic strength of the Hasmoneans caused Trypho to fear for his political future. When Jonathan demanded the rule over Akko (Ptolemais), Trypho realized the Hasmoneans posed a threat to his plan for a Syrian takeover of the entire Middle East. In Trypho's mind, the Hasmoneans had to be stopped. He arranged to meet Jonathan at Scythopolis, but when Jonathan arrived with a large army, Trypho realized he could not fight him openly. So Trypho decided to trap Jonathan through a cleverly devised plan of treachery. By making a number of concessions to Jonathan that would give him the rulership over Akko (Ptolemais), Trypho bribed him to accompany him to Akko with only a few fighting men from his large Hasmonean army. When Jonathan and his band arrived inside the walled city, the small fighting force was ambushed and slaughtered, as prearranged by Trypho. Only Jonathan was left alive to serve as a hostage for Trypho (see 1 Maccabees 12:39-48). Failing in his attempt to capture Jerusalem because of the stronger army of the Hasmoneans now under the leadership of Simon (Jonathan's brother), Trypho murdered Jonathan at the village of Bascama.

5. Graetz, *History of the Jews* 1:527.
6. Josephus, *Antiquities of the Jews* 12.10.6.
7. Ibid. 13.2.2.
8. Ibid. 13.2.3.
9. Dimont, *Jews, God and History*, 91.

Chapter 6

1. *Encyclopedia Judaica* 15:579-580.
2. Paul Johnson, *A History of the Jews* (New York: Harper & Row, 1987) 107.
3. George Foot Moore, *Judaism in the First Centuries of the Christian Era* (Cambridge: Harvard University Press, 1954) 1:56.
4. Josephus, *Antiquities of the Jews* 13.10.7.
5. Ibid. 13.8.4.
6. Solomon Zeitlin, *The Rise and Fall of the Jewish State* (Philadelphia: Jewish Publication Society, 1978) 1:344.
7. Ellison, *From Babylon to Bethlehem*, 66.
8. Josephus, *Antiquities of the Jews* 13.10.5.
9. See Talmud: Sotah 33a; Josephus, *Antiquities of the Jews* 13.10.7.
10. Josephus, *Antiquities of the Jews* 13.10.5.
11. See Talmud: Berakoth 29a; Josephus, *Antiquities of the Jews* 13.10.7.
12. Josephus, *Wars of the Jews* 1.5.2.
13. William Oesterley, H. Loewe, and Erwin I. J. Rosenthal, eds. *Judaism and Christianity*, 3 vols. (New York: Ktav, 1969) 2:318.
14. Josephus, *Antiquities of the Jews* 13.11.1.
15. Ibid. 13.2.3.
16. Bruce, *Israel and the Nations*, 175-176.
17. Josephus, *Antiquities of the Jews* 13.15.5.
18. ———, *Wars of the Jews* 13.15.5.
19. ———, *Antiquities of the Jews* 13.16.2.
20. Ibid. 13.16.1.
21. Ibid. 14.1.3.
22. Josephus, *Wars of the Jews* 1.6.3.
23. Graetz, *History of the Jews* 2:61.
24. Josephus, *Wars of the Jews* 1.7.6.
25. Ibid., 1.9.1.
26. Graetz, *History of the Jews* 2:77.
27. Ibid. 2:78.
28. Josephus, *Antiquities of the Jews* 14.9.4.
29. ———, *Wars of the Jews* 1.11.2.
30. Ibid. 1.11.8.
31. Graetz, *History of the Jews* 2:85-86.

32. Ibid. 2:95.
33. Josephus, *Antiquities of the Jews* 14.12.1.
34. Ibid. 16.3.3–4.6.
35. Ibid. 17.2.4-6.
36. Ibid. 17.6.5.
37. Ibid. 17.8.1-2.
38. Ibid. 17.6.3.
39. Ibid. 17.6.5.
40. Ibid.

Bibliography

Ben-Sasson, H.H., ed. *A History of the Jewish People.* Cambridge, MA: Harvard University Press, 1976.

Bromiley, Geoffrey W., ed. *The International Standard Bible Encyclopedia.* 4 vols. Grand Rapids: Eerdmans, 1986.

Bruce, F. F. *Israel and the Nations.* Grand Rapids: Eerdmans, 1963.

Cohen, Shaye J. D. *From the Maccabees to the Mishnah.* Philadelphia: Westminster, 1987.

Cornfeld, Gaalya, ed. *Josephus, The Jewish War.* Grand Rapids: Zondervan, 1982.

Dimont, Max I. *Jews, God and History.* New York: Penguin Books, Mentor Printing, 1994.

Durant, Will. *The Life of Greece.* New York: Simon and Schuster, 1939.

———. *The Story of Civilization.* New York: Simon and Schuster, 1935.

Edersheim, Alfred. *History of the Jewish Nation After the Destruction of Jerusalem Under Titus.* 1856. Revised edition, Grand Rapids: Baker, 1954.

Eerdman, Charles R. *The Book of Ezekiel: An Exposition.* Westwood, NJ: Revell, 1956.

Ellison, H.L. *From Babylon to Bethlehem.* Philadelphia: Westminster, 1979.

Encyclopedia Judaica. 16 vols. Jerusalem: Keter, 1972.

Epstein, I., ed. *The Babylonian Talmud.* London: Soncino, 1952.

Feinberg, Charles L. *Daniel: The Kingdom of the Lord.* Winona Lake, IN: B.M.H. Books, 1984.

Finkelstein, Louis, ed. *The Jews, Their History, Culture, and Religion.* Philadelphia: Jewish Publication Society, 1949.

Gaebelein, Arno C. *Gaebelein's Concise Commentary on the Whole Bible.* Neptune, NJ: Loizeaux, 1985.

———. *The Prophet Daniel.* New York: Our Hope, 1911.

Golub, Jacob S. *In the Days of the Second Temple.* Cincinnati: Union of American Hebrew Congregations, 1921.

Goodspeed, Edgar J., trans. *The Apocrypha.* New York: American Bible Society, n.d.

Graetz, Heinrich. *History of the Jews.* 6 vols. Philadelphia: Jewish Publication Society, 1967.

Grayzel, Solomon. *A History of the Jews.* Philadelphia: Jewish Publication Society, 1967.

Harrison, Roland K. *Introduction to the Old Testament.* Grand Rapids: Eerdmans, 1969.

Hengel, Martin. *Judaism and Hellenism.* trans. John Bowden. 2 vols. Philadelphia: Fortress, 1975.

Hutchins, Robert M., ed. *Great Books of the Western World.* Chicago: Benton, 1984.

Isaac, Benjamin. *The Limits of Empire, The Roman Army in the East.* New York: Oxford University Press, 1990.

Johnson, Paul. *A History of the Jews.* New York: Harper & Row, 1987.

La Sor, William Sanford. "1 and 2 Kings" in *The New Bible Commentary: Revised.* ed. D. Guthrie et al. Grand Rapids: Eerdmans, 1970.

Moore, George Foot. *Judaism in the First Centuries of the Christian Era.* 3 vols. Cambridge, MA: Harvard University Press, 1954.

Neusner, Jacob. *Judaism in the Beginning of Christianity.* Philadelphia: Fortress, 1984.

Oesterley, William, H. Loewe, and Erwin I. J. Rosenthal, eds. *Judaism and Christianity.* 3 vols. New York: Ktav, 1969.

Pfeiffer, Charles F. *Between the Testaments.* Grand Rapids: Baker, 1959.

Safrai, S. and M. Stern, eds. *The Jewish People in the First Century.* Philadelphia: Fortress, 1974.

Scherman, Nosson and Meir Zlotowitz. *History of the Jewish People, the Second Temple Era.* Brooklyn, NY: Mesorah Publications, 1982.

Schurer, Emil. *A History of the Jewish People in the Time of Jesus Christ.* ed. Nahum N. Glatzer. New York: Schocken, 1963.

Sevener, Harold A. *God's Man in Babylon—The Visions and Prophecies of Daniel.* Charlotte, NC: Chosen People Ministries, 1994.

Tatford, Frederick A. *The Climax of the Ages.* Grand Rapids: Zondervan, 1964.

Werblowsky, Zwi and Geoffrey Wigoder, eds. *Encyclopedia of the Jewish Religion.* New York: Adama, 1986.

Whiston, William, trans. *The Works of Flavius Josephus.* Grand Rapids: Associated Publishers and Authors, n.d.

Whyte, Alexander. *Bible Characters from the Old and New Testaments.* Grand Rapids: Kregel, n.d.

Zeitlin, Solomon. *The Rise and Fall of the Jewish State.* 3 vols. Philadelphia: Jewish Publication Society, 1978.